NUGGET

MAN OF THE CENTURY

Regarded as Australia's leading off-spinner, Ashley Mallett's ambition was to take 100 Test wickets, a feat he achieved in his twenty-third match, along with Shane Warne, Glenn McGrath and Graham McKenzie. As head of Spin Australia, an international spin-bowling coaching program, Ashley has worked with all of the leading modern spinners—including Shane Warne, Daniel Vettori and Monty Panesaar. In 2006, while establishing a spin bowling academy for the Sri Lanka Cricket Board in Colombo, he discovered the amazingly talented finger-flick bowler, Ajantha Mendis. Away from the cricket scene, Ashley lectures on biography writing at the Adelaide Centre for the Arts, TAFE, South Australia. *Nugget* is his 25th book.

MOSTLY BOOKS

Mitcham Square
Phone: (08) 8373 5190
nail: mostlybooks@internode.on.net

ALSO BY ASHLEY MALLETT

Rowdy

Spin Out

100 Cricket Tips

Master Sportsman Series. Cricket: *Don Bradman, Doug
Walters, The Chappells, Geoff Lawson, Kim Hughes,
Dennis Lillee, Rod Marsh, Allan Border.* Soccer: *John
Kosmina.* Tennis: *Evonne Cawley.* Australian Rules
Football: *Mark Williams, Wayne Johnston, Robert
Flower, Tim Watson*

Trumper, the illustrated biography

Clarrie Grimmett: the Bradman of spin

Bradman's Band

Eleven: the greatest eleven of the 20th century

The Black Lords of Summer

Chappelli Speaks Out

One of a Kind: the Doug Walters story

NUGGET

MAN OF THE CENTURY

The remarkable story of Nugget Rees,
Australian cricket's Peter Pan

ASHLEY MALLETT

ABC
Books

First published by ABC Books for the
AUSTRALIAN BROADCASTING CORPORATION
GPO Box 9994 Sydney NSW 2001

First published January 2009

National Library of Australia
Cataloguing-in-publication data

Mallett, Ashley, 1945
    Nugget: Man of the Century / Ashley Mallett
    1st ed.
    ISBN 978 0 7333 2409 3 (pbk.)
    Includes index
    Rees, Barry
    Cricket fans – Biography
    Cricket – Psychological aspects
    Achievement motivation
796.358092

Cover design by Luke Causby/Blue Cork Design
Typeset in 12 on 20pt Sabon by Kirby Jones
Front cover photograph by Ray Titus
Project management by Richard Smart Publishing
Printed and bound in Australia by Griffin Press

6 5 4 3 2

This book is dedicated to Nugget,

his family and to the memory of his proud,

loving father, Ray Rees.

Photographs

Forty, between pages 112 and 113

Nugget as a baby, child, growing up, and young man
Nugget with cricketers and footballers
Nugget on tour, and meeting the Queen
Nugget with relatives and friends
Nugget the boat captain, and dog lover
Nugget with even more friends
Nugget the cricketer, and masseur
Nugget the TV 'star'
Nugget, two cartoonists' views

Contents

Foreword   11

Preface   13

1 Introducing Nugget   15

2 From Barry to Nugget   34

3 Nugget's new world   58

4 Nugget meets the Queen   94

5 Nugget and cricket   117

6 Nugget and AFL   162

7 Nugget: A shining light   200

Index   235

Acknowledgements

Thanks to the following who helped me tell Nug's story:

Bruce Abernethy, Michael Atchison, Robin Bailhache, David Bartel, Geoff Barton*, Dr Donald Beard, Sue Bennie, Andy Bichel, Terry Blunden, Shane Bond, Troy Bond, Allan Border, Wally Bowyer*, Sir Donald Bradman*, Shayne Brewer, Dean Brogan, Jim Burke*, John Buchanan, Peter Burgoyne, Shaun Burgoyne, John Cahill, Josh Carr, Greg Chappell, Ian Chappell, Trevor Chappell, Michael Clarke, Reg Clements*, Stewart Cochrane, Chad Cornes, Kane Cornes, Lord (Sir Colin) Cowdrey*, Ken Cunningham, Chris Dittmar, Brett Ebert, Russell Ebert, Rob Elliot, Tim Evans, Les Favell*, George Fiacchi, Andrew Flintoff, Josh Francou, Ian Frazer, Eric Freeman, Paul Galloway*, Adam Gilchrist, Anna Gillespie, Tim Ginever, Phyllis Golding, Alan Greer, Wally Grout*, Joyce Guthrie, Neil Hawke*, Andrew Hilditch, Neil Harvey, Neville Hayes, Margaret Hayes, David Hookes*, Robyn Hookes, Michael Haysman, Bob Hawke, Ian Healy, Bob Hooper*, Kim Hughes, Merv Hughes, John Inverarity, Andrew Jarman, Mitchell Johnson, Harvey Jolly, Dean Jones, Michael Kasprowitz, Paula Keily, Adam Kingsley, Brendon Lade, Justin Langer, Stewart Law, Brett Lee, Martin Leslie, Bruce Light, Dennis Lillee, Gavin

Lincoln, Stuart MacGill, Devina Malcolm, Geoff Marsh, Rodney Marsh, Johnny Martin*, Tim May, Glenn McGrath, Tony McGuinness, Peter McIntyre, John McKinnon, Chris McDermott, Keith Miller*, Ron Mitchell, Geof Motley, Russell Moyle, Peter Motley, Tiny Nelson, Tim Nielsen, Max O'Connell, Norm O'Neill*, Wendy Page, David Parkinson, Sam Parkinson, Kylie Patching, Mike Perry, Michael Pettigrew, Matthew Primus, Barry Richards, Joan Richards, Matthew Richardson, Stephen Salopek, Sally Schultz, Steve Schultz, The Very Reverend Dr John Shepherd, Bob Simpson, Arthur Slee, Peter Sleep, Gladstone Small, Sir Garry Sobers, Jacob Surjen, Andrew Symonds, Brian Taber, Shaun Tait, Taylor Tannock, John Taylor (the Royal Page), Mark Taylor, Amye Tebbutt, Sachin Tendulkar, Charlie Thomas, Jeff Thomson, Warren Tredrea, Doug Walters, Doug Walters, Tom Warhurst*, Mark Waugh, Steve Waugh, Paul Weston, Fos Williams*, Mark Williams, Stephen Williams, Michael Woolley, Gavin Wanganeen, Shane Warne, Michael Wilson, Ted Wykes, Brad Young.

Thanks to Ben Mallett for conceptual text and marketing insights, and to my wife Christine for editing advice and the lovely back cover picture. The front cover picture was taken by Ray Titus. The pictures inside the book came from Nugget's collection, and from Stuart Dew, Pam Freeman, Barry Jarman, Wendy Page, Swan Richards, Diane Smith, and *The Advertiser*, Adelaide.

Deceased

Foreword

It was a call from the Anglican Dean of Perth, The Very Reverend Dr John Shepherd, 'Have I got a story for you!', that sent me on a wondrous journey into the exquisite world of Barry 'Nugget' Rees, a man cocooned deep in the inner sanctum of Australian cricket. Like many Australians, I had never heard of Nugget, so while Shepherd's call certainly intrigued me, I was sceptical. To meet the high *Australian Story* benchmark the story would need to transcend the ordinary. It did!

Much like Forrest Gump, Nugget is a simple, lovable character who became the improbable hero on an epic journey. Over the past five decades he has been included in many of Australian cricket's momentous occasions. He was an usher at Don Bradman's funeral; he carried the drinks during Steve Waugh's final game at the Sydney Cricket Ground; he was celebrating with the Australians in the dressing-room at Lord's in 1989 when they were on their way to regaining the Ashes.

———

It is a fantasy of all young cricketers to play in a team with their heroes. But for Nugget that fantasy is real—his dream is alive. Each season he pads up and plays a game against the South Australian State and Australian Test teams. Through the decades he's faced some of cricket's most famous bowlers— from the past, Alan Davidson, Garry Sobers, Dennis Lillee and Jeff Thomson, and more recently, Shane Warne, Glenn McGrath and Brett Lee. And as great sportsmen they've all embraced the fantasy; Nugget never fails to get a century.

But as you will discover in this book, it is what Nugget gives back to his sporting heroes that is so extraordinary. When I was producing the *Australian Story* about Nugget, former Test and first-class cricketer, John Inverarity told me, 'Australian cricketers are very protective of Nugget, and if anyone were ever to cause him harm, it would incur the wrath of a great many people.' I have no idea what the phenomenon is, but Nugget binds so many people together in an extraordinary, common bond of love for him.

As an *Australian Story* producer for more than twelve years, I have been involved with some very significant and memorable stories. And while it's impossible to nominate a favourite, I can honestly say (and this is a big call) that no story has given me greater joy than 'Man of the Century'. This is a story of great loyalty, comradeship and, above all, true Australian sportsmanship.

Wendy Page

Producer, *Australian Story*, ABC TV

Preface

Thank you Nugget for your company and friendship over the years and for your encouragement as I gradually put this book—your book—together. We shared many memorable days, often ending up at your spiritual football home, Alberton Oval. We walked and talked and laughed, meeting so many people I lost count. Nug, you gladden the hearts of the people you meet. You bring people down to earth and you make them smile.

Thanks also to Nugget's sisters, Diane and Pam, their husbands, Rusty and Neil, and their children, Corey and Cassie, and Rebecca, Cameron and Hamish. All gave of their time and provided words of love and respect for their beloved Nugget. Di and Pam gathered family photographs, cuttings and letters which all helped in weaving the fabric of Nug's story.

Ray Rees, Nugget's dad, died in 1988 and Nugget lives with Diane and Rusty in Colonel Light Gardens, near Adelaide. Ray Rees taught his only son, Barry, all about good manners and respect. Nugget learnt well and he respects everyone. Even today he calls his former employees at Rowe & Jarman Sports Store 'Mr Rowe and Mr Jarman'.

David 'Tidd' Rowe and Barry 'BJ' Jarman have watched Nugget's extraordinary transformation from a shy teenager to a unique man who became the veritable face of Rowe & Jarman Sports Store and 'much, much' more. Thanks Tidd, thanks BJ: champions both in the Nugget story.

Nugget loves his Test and State cricketers, Kensington Cricket Club, Port Magpies, Port Power and Goodwood Saints Football Club. For a time he showed affection towards the Adelaide Crows, but has kept quiet on that score since the Power made the AFL in 1997. Among a galaxy of sporting stars, Nugget continues to keep in contact with Shane Warne, Tim Nielsen, Darren 'Uncle Boof' Lehmann and Jason 'Dizzy' Gillespie. Tony McGuiness, champion footballer and once part-owner of Rowe & Jarman, has continued to be an important part of Nugget's life.

His long-time workmate Hans Ellenbroek, who taught Nugget all about becoming a football trainer, has been a wonderful friend. Nugget and I were so often together while gathering material for the book that Hans called us 'Laurel and Hardy'.

Everyone wanted to be involved in the telling of Nugget's story.

Ashley Mallett

CHAPTER 1

Introducing Nugget

Despite having the freedom to walk into the Australian Test cricket team dressing-room at Adelaide Oval at any time, Nugget always knocks on the door. He dresses immaculately, his hair brushed back; he never presumes.

Steve Waugh recalls: 'Every morning Nugget turns up to the ground. There's his knock on the door and he waits until someone says he can come in. His manners are great. He's like a beacon of goodness. Everyone lights up.'[1]

The room attendant Bob McDonald, an Irishman who always wears a neatly pressed white shirt and a permanent smile, welcomes Nugget.

'Morning Nugget, big match today?'

'Good morning, Bob. Yes, always a big day at Adelaide Oval.'

———

Earlier that day, over breakfast, Nugget's mobile phone rang. The caller was Shane Warne.

'Morning Nug. Hope you get down to the ground early. Punter [Ricky Ponting] said he wants Pigeon [Glenn McGrath] and me to bowl to you. He said if we can bowl well to you, the Poms are no chance. Remember to bring your gloves, Nugget.'

Within a few minutes Nugget will be central to good-natured banter in the Australian dressing-room. It is always tense, especially the first morning of a big game. Apart from the Test players, team coaches and management, and the odd room attendant, no-one gains entry to the Australian dressing-room during a Test match. No-one, that is, other than Barry 'Nugget' Rees.

Nugget walks about the room, shaking hands with the players and patting them on the shoulder. They are all glad to see him. Adam Gilchrist hugs him. Mike Hussey hands him a Coke Zero. Michael Clarke yells from the corner, 'You look good for a hundred today, Nugget.'

Doc Beard puts a gentle hand on Nugget's shoulder. 'Hope all the players are okay, Nugget.'

'Oh yes, Doc. I watched them train yesterday. Everyone is fit and Warney's about to do something special, you'll see.'

Dr Donald Beard served in the Australian Army in Korea in 1950–51 as a medical officer before further studies saw him become a surgeon, and in 1968 he spent five months as the leading medic in the First Australian Army Field

Hospital in Vietnam. For more than 40 years Doc Beard was the South Australian Cricket Association's medical officer and he came to rely on Nugget's perception of the passing parade of South Australian and Australian cricketers.

'Nugget is the most amazing person I've met,' the Doc says. 'In all the years I've been with the SACA Nugget was never wrong with one of his concerns. Nugget would say, "Doc, you'd better have a look at so and so, I think he's depressed." He was right that time and every other occasion.'[2]

Late in the 1971–72 Australian summer, Nugget went to Doc Beard and said, 'Doc, I think you'd better have a look at Ian Chappell. He has a nasty wound on his chest.'

Unbeknown to the Doc, after Australia's victory over England in the First Test at Old Trafford in June 1968, the players were skylarking in the showers and mystery spinner John Gleeson stubbed a cigarette on Ian's chest. That was three years before he noticed a disturbing change in the colour of the tissue right on that very spot. The wound turned out to be cancerous and Doc Beard removed it only days before Chappell led the 1972 Australian tour of England.

Confident that Ricky Ponting's men are fit and well and rearing to go, Doc Beard shakes Nugget's hand and moves away. Nugget continues to greet the players, making sure that he misses no-one. Nugget is even more excited than the hundreds of kids rushing towards the entrance in time to watch the first ball of the Test.

How those kids would have loved to be in Nugget's shoes for a day.

Nugget dresses quickly—Jason Gillespie's shirt, Mark Taylor's creams, Brett Lee's socks and boots.

'Thanks Dizzy, Tubby and Binga—a great team effort,' he says aloud.

Then, with the greatest reverence, he dons his coveted baggy-green cap—the one Barry Jarman gave him many years ago.

In the wake of having greeted everyone in the room, some more than once, Nugget finds his hands soaked with perspiration. He puts on his gloves and joins Ricky Ponting at the top of the stairs outside the Australian dressing-room.

The two men shake hands. As they walk purposefully down the stairs of the Members' Stand, Nugget is all too aware that he is following in the footsteps of the greats: Don Bradman, Bill Ponsford, Clem Hill, Ian and Greg Chappell, Harold Larwood, Victor Trumper, Vic Richardson, Clarrie Grimmett, Bill O'Reilly, Ray Lindwall, and his early hero, the man after whom he is nicknamed, Keith 'Nugget' Miller.

'I see you fully expect to bat today, Nugget,' Ponting laughs, noting that Nugget is wearing pads and gloves.

'Yes, Punter. I'm confident of winning the toss, much, much...'

Nugget wears a big smile, so too Ponting and the thousands of people who pack the lush green of Adelaide Oval. Nugget and Ponting again shake hands in the middle of the famous ground where match referee Clive Lloyd greets them. Lloyd hands the specially minted gold coin to Ricky Ponting.

'Thanks Clive,' Ponting says. He looks over at Nugget. 'Ready, mate?'

Nugget gives the thumbs up.

Ponting holds the coin in the crook of his thumb. Like the opening bounce of the AFL Grand Final at the MCG, all eyes are on the gold coin tossed high into the air. The coin falls on the freshly cut grass, just off the pitch and Lloyd moves to check. He turns the coin over in his hand and smiles, for he discovers that Nugget's profile adorns both sides of the coin.

Nugget cuts and drives with his customary precision and power. His score climbs rapidly and when he reaches 96 there is a thunderous appeal for lbw from Brett Lee.

Nugget's heart misses a beat, but he is calmed when Adam Gilchrist shows no interest from behind the wicket and a split-second later a smile breaks across his cheery face when umpire Billy Bowden keeps his crooked right index finger by his side. The batsman survives.

Moments later, a deft Nugget leg-glance off Andrew Symonds' bowling brings three more runs, giving him the strike. He then faces the first ball of Stuart Clarke's over and launches into a splendid cover drive, the ball racing across the turf like a scurrying rabbit and into the picket fence in front of the Members' Stand. Nugget has his century, bringing unanimous applause.

Ponting rushes to Nugget's side and thrusts out his right hand in congratulation. 'Great stuff, mate. Hey, that's my bat. The one I gave you last year after my Test hundred against India here.'

'Yes, Punter,' Nugget smiles. 'And including this one today, I've already scored five centuries with your old bat!'

Nugget acknowledges the crowd with humility and calmness which belies the excitement within. He waves his bat to all sections of the ground then disappears up the race and into the confines of the Australian dressing-room. He is clapped off the field by the entire Australian team and Nugget tells the boys, 'a standing aviation, much, much'. (In Nugget-speak, 'aviation' means 'ovation'.) Another century under the belt and Nugget takes off his helmet and carefully places his batting gear in his green and gold Australian bag, the one which has Nugget Rees superimposed over the name Matthew Hayden.

For 45 years Nugget has been thrashing the life out of some of the greatest bowlers to walk the Test stage. Garry Sobers, Dennis Lillee, Jeff Thomson, Glenn McGrath, Shane Warne and Brett Lee have all been belted about Adelaide Oval by Nugget, whose body shape and batting style is so reminiscent of the great England batsman Colin Cowdrey. Nugget has a better batting average than Don Bradman and he has scored so many centuries that he has amassed more than the 54, 211 runs that W.G. Grace scored in his career which spanned more than 30 years.

It has become traditional for the Australian players to join Nugget in the all-important 'Test' within a Test match. And all the players get a huge thrill from watching the joy Nugget derives from scoring runs at every outing.

At the end of these impromptu matches, Nugget immediately gears himself for a different, albeit just as important, role. Before the Test men move onto the Adelaide Oval, Nugget delivers a motivational address. Nugget has been giving these stirring speeches for as long as the locusts have eaten. He has fired up teams led by such brilliant captains as Les Favell, Richie Benaud, Ian Chappell and Mark Taylor. Now it's Ricky Ponting's turn.

It takes a knowing nod and cricket's Peter Pan clambers onto the table in the centre of the Australian dressing-room. Stuart Clarke stretches in a corner, Matthew Hayden is on his haunches, Brett Lee limbers up and Ricky Ponting sits by his locker—a moment of contemplation before leading his men into battle.

'C'mon fellas,' Nugget says, 'just ten wickets this session. Bowlers back up the fieldsman...' Nugget looks about the room and catches Ricky Ponting's eye. The Australian captain winks at him. 'Now c'mon Brett Lee. In the Sydney Test you bowled half-rat power. Stuart Clarke is bowling twice as fast. Lift your game Binga!'

With a mischievous glint in his eye, Andrew Symonds calls out, 'Hey, Nugget. What about Haydos' fielding?'

Nugget stares at Matthew Hayden. 'Yes, Haydos, get real, eh? Catch 'em Haydos, catch 'em, okay? C'mon Haydos, concentrate out there!'

There is spontaneous applause and the room is filled with laughter. Nugget has spoken. The players, uplifted by Nugget's words, move briskly from the room and most of them are still laughing when they hit the surface of Adelaide Oval. Fired-up, Brett Lee bowls like a human hurricane and puts the wind up the Poms.

But Nugget didn't see a lot of the first session. All the chairs around the table had been removed and he was left marooned on the very platform from which he delivered his stirring speech.

Ian Chappell was perhaps the first Test captain to fully realise the value of Nugget in the dressing-room. He saw the warmth and loyalty which simply exudes from the man. As Steve Waugh said recently: 'You feel as if you've got another player on your team. Inside our dressing-room we had Nugget, a hero of our own. A guy that embodied the spirit and very essence of the baggy-green and represented the passion of the supporters.'[3]

Former WA, SA and Test batsman John Inverarity says the team dynamic that exists in every elite cricket team dressing-room is greatly enhanced by the presence of Nugget: 'There is a certain chemistry and Nugget enhances that chemistry within the team dynamic. Nugget is part of the bond between the players of the past and the current crop. The State and Test players love Nugget. They are fiercely protective of him and he of them.'[4]

From the moment Adam Gilchrist first came to Adelaide to play for Australia, he found Nugget a revelation. Gilchrist says: 'Seeing the effect Nugget has in the team environment, it touched me, and I went away feeling better about myself. The simplicity of the man, how simply he looks at things and explains things, it's just so pure and honest. It's wonderful, a refreshing thing to happen in life. He teaches us all a little about respect, about honesty and loyalty. He is one of the most honest, open, loyal, respectful human beings you'll ever meet.

'Once, after we'd won a game, Nugget stood on the table to say a few words. He'd had his light beer and lemonade in helping us celebrate and he said, "Thank you, thank you, much, much" many times. Then he looked about the room and looked at each of the players and he said, "Thank you, you've made me feel really, really good". I just wanted to grab him and hug him and say, "No mate, it's the other way around. What you have done for us and what you have brought to our life—it's extraordinary. So thank you, Nugget."'[5]

For the past 27 years Nugget has been asking me to write his story. In 2006 he approached me at Adelaide Oval. Resplendent in his Redbacks kit, SA cap and tracksuit, with an official Cricket Australia player security card dangling round his neck, Nugget's face beamed as he held out his hand in greeting.

'Hey Rowdy, when are you going to write that book on me?' he asked. There was urgency in his voice and I took care to jot down his contact numbers. Writing a book about the life and times of Barry 'Nugget' Rees wasn't high on my list of priorities at that time; however, when I sat down to watch the ABC's *Australian Story* program on February 19, 2007, I was immediately grabbed by the emotion.

Australian Story produced a fitting tribute to a man who has touched the lives of many. Entitled 'Man of the Century', the story captured the imagination of a nation. Cricket and AFL people throughout the land already knew and loved Nugget. But now millions of Australians had an insight into a man of great honesty and loyalty, a man of warm heart, who exudes pure love, a man who epitomises all that is good.

It hit me like a tidal wave and in my mind there was Nugget telling me over and over, 'There, you see, Rowdy. I tell ya—it's time to write my story'.

When Adam Gilchrist learnt about the book on Nugget, he wrote: 'A brilliant idea and a truly inspiring topic. As you know, in the elite sporting world many blokes get carried away with the limelight but, unbeknown to him, Nugget has that unique ability to ground us and make us realise we are normal humans who happen to play cricket well. I love having that type of influence around and the irony happens because he idolises the boys so much.'[6]

So I flew to Sydney to interview *Australian Story* producer Wendy Page and discovered that her interest in Nugget was sparked by a man of the cloth, The Very Reverend Dr John Shepherd, Anglican Dean of Perth.

Former SA and Test batsman and now national selector Andrew Hilditch, who has taken Nugget under his wing over recent years, invites Nugget to accompany him interstate to matches where he runs an eye over the emerging talent in State cricket. Sometimes it is a one-day international, but always, each summer, Hilditch takes Nugget to a big game or two. On a trip to watch the South Australian Redbacks play the Western Australian Warriors in Perth, Hilditch took Nugget along to former WA, SA and Australian batsman John Inverarity's home for dinner.

Among the guests was Dr John Shepherd. He recalls: 'Meeting Nugget that night was wonderful. I thought him to be a brilliant character and I was immediately struck by the warmth and sincerity of the man. I marvelled how Hilditch and Inverarity, both former international cricketers, were so respectful and loving toward Nugget.

'I quizzed Nugget on the game. "Hey, Nugget, was Don Tallon a better keeper than Barry Jarman?" Quick as a flash Nugget replied that both were fine batsman-wicket-keepers, but he wouldn't compare them. He said they are both good players.'[7]

The Anglican Dean of Perth straightaway picked up Nugget's aura of peace and love and humility. Nugget is a spiritual soul, radiating light and positive vibration. Dr Shepherd says, 'It's like Nugget is already in heaven. He exudes joy and love and those lucky enough to meet him are being given an idea of what we can expect in the after-life: Here he stands; the happy, smiling messenger angel giving us a foretaste of what lies in store.

'The day after meeting Nugget, I rang Wendy and told her that she simply had to do a feature on him. That was some nine months before the show was aired.'[8]

Wendy Page got into journalism at the age of 43 and that is considered 'late' in the helter-skelter media world. She joined the *7.30 Report* as a researcher and soon became a producer. In 1996 she joined *Australian Story* as one of the inaugural producers of the program. During her lengthy stint with the show, Wendy has produced many ground-breaking stories. One of these was the case of John Button whom *Australian Story* brought face-to-face with the family of the girl he had been wrongly convicted of murdering in 1963. Together with Ian Harley, in 2002 Wendy won her first Walkley Award, Australia's top media award for excellence in journalism, for this story.

It was this same story about John Button which first brought her into contact with The Very Reverend Dr John Shepherd. At Wendy's request he had conducted a beautiful memorial service for the girl who had been murdered four decades earlier. Dr Shepherd was subsequently the guest presenter for another of Wendy's stories. So when Dr Shepherd called her about Nugget, saying, 'Wendy, I have the best story for you', she knew it would be a special one.[9]

Wendy recalls: 'I eventually flew to Perth and met John Inverarity. He was initially wary and very protective of Nugget. He was concerned that the notoriety and celebrity status Nugget would get from the feature might impact in a negative way.

The story of Nugget captured my interest. The problem was the cricket season was over and if the story was to proceed I would need to film it during the cricket season. So, I filed it away in my mind for the next year, hoping nobody else would get to it. I needn't have worried because it had been sitting for decades right under the noses of many sports journalists.

'The next summer I ran the idea past my boss and she said, "Go for it!" However, it's one thing to have a great story idea, but you also need people willing to appear on camera to tell the story.

'Just after Christmas I was on my way to our farm in Tasmania so I went via Adelaide to meet Nugget and his family. Like everyone else I simply fell in love with him straightaway and I knew then the story would work.'[10]

When filming began Wendy saw the great love and respect which abounded between Nugget and the Australian cricket players—an indefinable bond of love and respect. She recalls that when Adam Gilchrist heard that *Australian Story* planned to run a feature on Nugget, he contacted her and offered to be in the program. Gilchrist's offer was among many fascinating heart-warming aspects that emerged as Wendy put the story together, and *Australian Story* filmed tributes to Nugget from other cricket luminaries including Dennis Lillee and Steve Waugh.

SA Captain and Test batsman Darren Lehmann was the guest presenter for Nugget's *Australian Story*: 'After winning the Ashes recently, the Australian cricket team was the toast of the nation, but they've also got a hero of their own, a bloke you've probably never heard of. He's one of my best mates.

'Barry "Nugget" Rees has inspired the cricketing elite of Australia for nearly five decades. This is his story...'[11]

According to Wendy: 'The most amazing thing is, I was astounded to witness generations of Australian cricketing heroes being so openly affectionate and protective towards one special human being. These men hug Nugget. Their affection for him is very real. That was the thing which really blew me away.'[12]

But, as Wendy discovered, Nugget's remarkable place in Australian cricket was not widely known: 'When I was working out of the ABC offices in Adelaide, I found all the sports reporters knew of Nugget, but I was amazed they had no idea how deeply entrenched Nugget was in the cricket world. I think they just saw him as a mascot (something which the cricketers vehemently reject) and they had no idea of the depth of feeling the top cricketers and footballers in South Australia had for Nugget. That really surprised me.'[13]

The night before Nugget was featured on *Australian Story*, his sister, Diane, rang Wendy with concerns about the program. Wendy says: 'With almost every story we do, the people who are featuring on the program go into a panic just before we go to air'. Di was suddenly worried that the program would adversely offend Nugget.

'In the lead-up publicity to the show, a journalist had described Nugget as being intellectually disabled which really distressed the family. In reality Nugget might be a bit slow in some areas—aren't we all—but within him there is a genius. It is sad that people need to find a label for others. To me Nugget is part Rain Man, part Forest Gump.[14]

Fortunately, Wendy was able to allay Di's fears and was given her blessing for the show to go ahead.

The nation loved Nugget's story. The Australian cricketers also loved it and each player was given a CD of the program. Adam Gilchrist believed 'Man of the Century' inspired him to his brilliant 149 which virtually won Australia the World Cup.

On 22 February, 2007, a couple of days after the show aired in Australia, Wendy Page wrote to Nugget:

Dear Nugget,

You are my most special story ever. How lucky I was that The Very Rev. Dr. John Shepherd, the Dean of Perth, met you at John Inverarity's home. I will always remember his phone call the next day, saying what a wonderful person you are and that I should do a story about you. And here we are a year later with an absolute triumph!

The audience absolutely LOVED it, as I am sure you well know from the response you have been getting. Thank you so much for allowing me into your life. I know there were times when you probably got fed up with us being around, but it seems it was all worth it in the end.

Looking forward to seeing you in Sydney next year, or whenever. And I'll see you in Adelaide one day.

With my very best wishes and I'll be watching the World Cup with much greater interest than I ever would have before! I think you've got me hooked.

Sincerely,

(Signed)

Wendy Page

Producer, *Australian Story*

Accolades flooded in. For Wendy Page, the story won her a second Walkley Award for journalistic excellence, winning the Sport Feature Coverage. 'Man of the Century' (Wendy Page, producer, and Ian Harley, editor) was also short-listed as a finalist in the prestigious New York Festivals of Film awards. Nugget has framed copies of both these awards in his special memorabilia room at home.

The *Australian Story* feature made Barry 'Nugget' Rees

an instant hero among the masses. Millions of Australians got to know the Nugget who has been embraced by Test cricketers and AFL footballers. They were taken into Nugget's special world—a world of joy and love.

At St Arnaud Primary School in Victoria, the leadership group of Year 5 and 6 students were given a task by school principal Mark McLay to do a worksheet on Nugget's life. After watching *Australian Story*'s 'Man of the Century', they were asked to write 'Five things about Nugget' and to answer the question 'Is Nugget a leader?'

The kids' consensus was that Nugget was 'reliable, encouraging, a good role model and there was not a mean bone in his body'. Collectively, they all sensed the great goodness that emanated from Nugget. His spirit touched them.

In agreeing that Nugget was a leader, Kylie Patching wrote: 'Nugget encourages people, he sets a good example. He has a sense of humour, he is reliable, a good motivator and he cares for and loves everyone.'

Amye Tebbutt wrote that Nugget 'is a leader because if someone went out [dismissed playing cricket] he would always say something to cheer them up. Nugget knows where he can push the boys to and he knows when to stop.'

Taylor Tannock wrote that Nugget only says nice things about people: 'I think if everyone in the world was like Nugget we would have a great world full of friendly people.'[15]

After the *Australian Story* feature, Nugget and his family received an avalanche of emails, letters, cards and presents from an extraordinary cross-section of well-wishers. Nugget gives of himself in every waking moment and that spirit of giving came through loud and clear in 'Man of the Century'. In that same spirit of giving, Barbara Brown of Dover Gardens knitted a teddy bear, in Port Power colors, and sent the present to the Port Adelaide Football Club, knowing that her gift would find Nugget.

Former SA and Test wicket-keeper Barry Jarman, who has had an extraordinary impact on the life of Nugget, sums up Nugget's effect on all who know him: 'You know, if someone today saw Nugget sitting beside Queen Elizabeth, they'd say, "Who's the lady sitting beside Nugget?"'[16]

Nugget is a story about an uncomplicated man of great passion and love. It is about his cricket and football adventures; the way he generates respect, loyalty and good manners.

In his own special way, Nugget touches the heart of humanity.

Nugget's life is a love story.

Notes

1   Steve Waugh, *Australian Story*, February 2007
2   Dr Donald Beard to author, July 2007
3   Steve Waugh, *Australian Story*, February 2007
4   John Inverarity, *Australian Story*, February 2007
5   Adam Gilchrist to author, 2008
6   Adam Gilchrist in email to author, dated June 21, 2007
7   The Very Reverend Dr John Shepherd, Anglican Dean of Perth, to author, February 2008
8   ibid.
9   Wendy Page to author, Sydney, January 2008
10 ibid.
11 Darren Lehmann introducing Nugget on *Australian Story*, February 2007
12 Wendy Page to author, Sydney, January 2008
13 ibid.
14 ibid.
15 Extracts of comments by Year 5 and 6 leadership group students at St Arnaud Primary School, Victoria
16 Barry Jarman to author, July 2007

CHAPTER 2

From Barry to Nugget

Barry William Rees was born at The Memorial Hospital, North Adelaide, on February 28, 1944. The firstborn to Ray and Mary Rees, Barry has two younger sisters, Pam, born in 1947, and Diane, who arrived in 1951.

A war baby, Barry came into the world a week before the Allies began daily bombing raids over Berlin. At birth he was a bonny, bouncing 6 pounds 10 ounces. The day Barry was born, Mary Rees was handed a card detailing a list of requisites, 'For Mother', 'For Baby'.

Barry William Rees' 'For Baby' list included:

- 1 cake of Johnson's Baby Soap
- 2½ dozen napkins
- 6 gowns

———

- 4 knitted pillows
- 3 woollen singlets
- 4 cotton singlets
- 2 flannelette binders
- 2 A-wraps
- 4 pairs bootees

Napkins were to be laundered at the hospital for a weekly fee of 1s 6d. A further 2s 6d was charged for baby Barry's pharmaceutical needs and £1 0s 1d. for all sterilisation.

For the first week, the hospital allowed Mary only two visitors: her proud husband Ray and her mother.

Telegrams and letters began to flow into the Rees household. A telegram from Sydney-based family friends, Gwen and John Evennett, arrived a couple of days after the birth.

> 6. MOSMAN NSW 16 9.45A ILO.
> Mrs Rees
> Memorial Hospital, North Adelaide, SA
> Congratulations to son on choice of parents love
> The Evenetts.

On the back of the envelope which held the telegram were the words 'Loose Lips Sink Ships', a stark reminder to all that there was still a war going on.

Another family friend, Vera, who lived at nearby Myrtle Bank, wrote to Mary: 'I like "Barry" and the William Rees is quite manly. What a sheik to be.'

While Winfred, of Firle, wrote: 'You managed things rather well having your infant on the 28th, not the 29th. It would have been very sad if he only had a birthday every four years.'

Barry's Uncle Bill, Ray's brother, revealed the humorous side of the family: 'By the time this note reaches you, Barry will be four days old, and would be recognised as one of the old stagers in the Nursery.

'It is Ray's intention to take your white purse out to the Trots tomorrow and attempt to double it—don't let on to him that I have passed this on.'

By March 24, 1944, less than a month later, Barry weighed 8 pounds 7 ounces. Doctor Munday, the obstetrician at the Memorial Hospital, noted on the Mother's Card of the local Mothers and Babies Health Association that breast-fed Barry Rees needed 'no dummy' but required 'warm boiled water between feeds'.

By September 29, 1944, Barry weighed in at a healthy 20 pounds 4 ounces. In the special remarks column it was noted: 'Vegetable puree and broth. Two teaspoons before 2pm feed. Raw egg yolk, 3 drops.'

The Rees family lived in Colonel Light Gardens on West Park Way in a Californian bungalow so typical of the suburb. Colonel Light Gardens, some 6 km from Adelaide, is

Australia's most complete example of an early 1900s garden suburb, known for its radial street pattern, landscaped reserves and gardens, and wide tree-lined avenues. In 1924, under the State Government's 'Thousand Homes Scheme', it was anticipated that houses in Colonel Light Gardens would be bought by the returned soldiers of World War I and working-class civilians with a ceiling sale price of £700. A large hall was erected by the Rechabite Lodge in 1929, which has been owned by the RSL since 1945. Also in 1929 the Colonel Light primary and infant schools were built. Colonel Light Gardens retained autonomy from local government control until 1975 (the same year Nugget celebrated Ian Chappell's SA team winning the Sheffield Shield), when it was proclaimed a part of the Mitcham District Council.

Barry used to ride his tricycle to Colonel Light Gardens School and on his way he dropped Pam at kindergarten. Pam stood on the rear axle and held on for dear life as Barry pedalled along the footpath, with his leather school satchel hanging from behind the seat.

'Barry was always protective of me and Diane,' Pam says. 'He was wonderful. After school he would pick me up, ensuring that I got home safely.

'One day, when Barry was seven and I was four years old, he took me on the five-minute walk to the local Mothers and Babies Association hall to see a visiting magician perform. All the kids in the neighbourhood must have been there, for the place was packed. There we were sitting cross-legged on the floor as the magician went about his stuff, pulling scarves out of a hat and the like. Then he started talking about "making people disappear" and cutting things. I got very upset and started screaming. Barry put his arm around me and consoled me. Then he took me home to Mum and Dad and explained how the magician had scared me. Barry then announced that he was going back to "see the end of the show".[1]

Adelaide in the 1950s was a time of innocence. On those still, hot nights of summer, people slept under the stars on mattresses placed on their front lawns. Front doors were left unlocked and car keys were left in cars parked on the street outside their homes. Of course, the odd car was stolen, but in those days car theft was rare.

Pam recalls: 'We kids were allowed to go anywhere during the day time, but the golden rule was always to be home before dark.

'One day Barry and I went out with friends. I think we went to pick mushrooms or something. It got quite late and Janet—the most senior among the children and the self-appointed leader—urged me to join her for the walk home rather than go with Barry "because you'll get lost".

'I went with Janet but by the time I got home it was dark and Dad, with a face like thunder, was waiting at the front gate. Barry came to my rescue and saved me from the strap by explaining to Dad and Mum that Janet had insisted I go with her. He was always helping me out.'[2]

Mary Rees loved flowers and when Pam was out one day with Barry, they came across a garden full of beautiful blooms. 'I was only about four years old and very tiny. The flowers seemed enormous to me,' Pam remembers. 'Barry warned me not to touch the flowers, but a girl who was with us urged me to start picking them and as we frantically collected the flowers, a woman appeared. She had a bit of a reputation in the area for being a bit of a witch, an ogre, someone to be avoided. She was very agitated. Barry walked up to her and I don't know what he said to her but she quickly retreated from sight, wagging her finger at me as she departed. As we slipped away I admired the beautiful flowers I had picked for Mum.'[3]

Every Sunday in summer Barry, Pam and Diane would pile into the family car with their parents and head for Somerton Beach. There they played beach cricket. On Sundays at other times of the year, the Rees family headed for a national park where they had a permanent tennis court booking. 'We didn't have a lot of money,' Pam says, 'but we had a helluva lot of fun.'[4]

Ray Rees loved his cars. The first one the children can remember was an Austin with a canvas roof, but the car that was their father's pride and joy was a cream-coloured, 6-cylinder, 4-door saloon: a Vauxhall Velox. 'Dad had Barry and me washing the car at least once a week. Dad was very particular about the car's condition,' Pam says.[5] Not surprisingly the Vauxhall Velox was in pristine condition.

Barry's love of sport began in those early days of his childhood. He used to go to the local football with his father, Ray, and his uncle Bill. They were keen Port Adelaide Football Club fans. His dad also took Nugget to the cricket and they watched matches at the Adelaide Oval—Sheffield Shield games and annual Test matches. It was here that Barry first saw the superb all-round talent of Keith 'Nugget' Miller, Barry's early cricket hero.

As Chairman of the SA Trotting Association, Ray Rees also made every Saturday night a night to remember for his family at the Wayville trotting track. While their father busied himself having a bet and mixing with punters, owners and trainers, Barry, Pam and Diane sat in the grandstand. They watched the horses and ate fish and chips out of newspaper wrapping.

They would also regularly visit their 'uncle' Wal W.C. Bowyer (a family friend and a trainer of trotters) at his place in Woodville and look at the horses in the stables. Pam recalls: 'I remember one particular horse—Radiant Robert. He was apparently a very good horse, but Dad called him a "mean bugger" and he told us not to go anywhere near him.

'When we got to his stall the horse took one look at me and he put his ears back; I could see the whites of his eyes. His nostrils flared and he glared at me. I backed off, but Barry walked up slowly and confidently. He put out his right hand, offering him a carrot, and the horse gratefully accepted the food and licked Barry's hand. Radiant Robert was like a little lamb in the hands of my gorgeous big brother, Barry.'[6]

Radiant Robert was, in fact, a mighty pacer. He won the South Australian Derby and the Victorian Derby, in addition to a number of cup races and free-for-alls in SA. He was also a successful stallion at stud. Ron Mitchell, who lived in Woodville in the 1950s and who also owned the brilliant SA pacer of the 1990s, Robber John, says that Radiant Robert sired 211 foals and 92 of them won races.[7]

But for the Rees children, visits to Wally Bowyer's stables was about having fun. Pam says, 'Our uncle Wal gave Barry racing colours and we'd go home after the trots and emulate the races. There was Barry in his colours with the riding whip and I was the horse, a skipping rope doubled as a gig. At the end of the action Barry always told me that I was a "good horse" and as a reward for being a "good horse", he gave me a carrot.'[8]

Barry was often given the reins at Wally Bowyer's track. He says, 'Uncle Wal used to get me to ride the gig around the track. I was okay with that—I liked the horses and they never seemed to play up at all.'

Even as a young child Pam Rees began to realise that her big brother, Barry, had a special quality about him. 'He was gentle and kind and he was very protective of his sisters. Barry also had, from the very early days, a fabulous sense of humour. Barry could laugh at himself and we all laughed with him.'[9]

Barry's childhood was a happy and contented one, with a family life of backyard barbecues, Sundays at the beach or playing tennis in the hills, and fun times at the trots. But it all came to a tragic end when Mary Rees, who had been fighting ill-health, passed away on September 29, 1956. She was only 36 years old.

Pam says the time of their mother's death was so traumatic that it spelt the virtual end of their childhood. 'Some twelve months leading up to Mum's passing, we were living away from home with a variety of relatives. I remember cooking a roast around that time and I was still only nine years old. I think Dad leant on me in some ways. Like us all I think he was a bit lost without Mum.'[10]

Paula Keily knew the Rees family well. Her husband, Keith, worked with Ray's brother, Bill Rees, at the Wadlow Timber Company in Alberton. Ray, Keith and Bill were all accountants, and all were fond of horse racing.

'I so remember dear Nugget,' Paula says. 'He was a beautiful baby and he's a lovely man. I suppose I had more to do with the two girls, Pam and Diane. The whole family so loved their mother. Mary was very sick for a long period. She was only young yet in the last few years of her life she couldn't even walk up a hill. Mary died so young, she was only 36. Mary had rheumatic fever as a child and that illness greatly affected her heart. Mary's brother, Les Roberts, died only a couple of years back. He was in his nineties.'[11]

Joyce and Eric Guthrie were great friends of the Rees

family. Eric Guthrie also worked at Wadlows, where he was in charge of the milling, and he was good mates with Ray and Bill Rees. Joyce says: 'In the last couple of months of Mary's life, their girls, Pam and Diane, came to live with us and Barry went to live with his uncle Bill.

'Barry was a beautiful boy and he has developed into a lovely man. Eric gave him the nickname "Champ", short for "Champion", and we always called him "Champ".

'Barry was just like he is today, so well-mannered—he always stood up if a lady walked into the room. And he has now what he had as a young boy, an incredible memory.'[12]

But his mother's death hit Barry very hard: 'Mum was sick for a long time. I don't know whether I went to her funeral. I don't think so. I miss her very much. I remember her well. She was a lovely lady.'

Barry's father, Ray Rees, always set an example for his children to follow. 'Our dad was very much a true gentleman,' Diane says. 'Very proper.'[13]

Ray was born in 1916, to William Griffith Rees and Isabel Beatrice Maud Rees, while his younger brother, William John Troy Rees, was born in August 1918. Ray was educated at Croydon Primary School where he was dux of each class until Grade 7 and gained the highest marks in the Qualifying Entrance Examination—674 out of a possible 700.

He attended Woodville High School from 1929 to 1934, where he was head prefect and captain of the cricket and football teams. In his school record for 1931, Ray scored very well in all the categories. His trustworthiness was 'excellent'; his qualities of leadership were 'very good'; his disposition was 'serious, earnest, steady' and his deportment and neatness were 'very good'. The headmaster, Mr J. Gluis, wrote a personal note: 'Ray is a very willing and diligent worker, always courteous and gentlemanly... He is possessed of very good abilities and is absolutely honourable. I have pleasure in highly recommending him.'[14]

Ray Rees left school in 1934. He worked for the stock exchange before transferring to share broker F.J. Wimble for two years. Ray then worked for A.E.H. Evans and Company, chartered accountants, in Grenfell Street, Adelaide. He was later a senior partner of the firm.

A licensed liquidator, auditor, registered tax agent (for 43 years) and Justice of the Peace (45 years), Ray was Chairman of the South Australian Trotting Control Board from 1973 to 1984; and during his term of office Ray introduced freeze branding, which became a national practice, and the 2 for 1 handicapping system. He was a member of the SA Totalizator Agency Board and served as Vice President and Treasurer of the Inter-Dominion Trotting Council from 1973 to 1984. He was also a member of the Australian Harness Racing Council, and a member of the South Australian Cricket Association for 47 years.

Ray floated the first public-listed uranium and oil companies in Australia—Lakes Entrance (now known as

Woodside Petroleum) and Uranium Development Prospecting Company. He was the Chief Executive Officer for the Home for Incurables (now called the Julia Farr Centre) for 37 years, and during the time he was there the home became the largest of its type in the Southern Hemisphere. He was on the board of a host of companies, including Eagle Star Insurance, Oil Investment Limited, Mintaro, Slate Flagstone Limited and SA Enamel Group of Companies.

Ray Rees married Mary Roberts in September 1940 and they had sixteen happy years together. He was distraught when his wife passed away.

Immediately following their mother's death was a time of trauma and confusion for the children. 'There were lots and lots of housekeepers. They'd come and they'd go,' Diane says.[15]

Much to the dismay of his three children, Ray Rees ultimatey married his housekeeper, Theresa Ruess, on March 9, 1964.

Pam's says, 'Theresa was good-looking. Dad was lonely and pretty well off, so you can form your own conclusions...'[16]

Nugget doesn't hold back: 'Dad didn't really want to marry her, I know. He did it to keep us together as a family.'

Their stepmother was German, a daughter of Herr Peter and Frau Theresa Doeppel of Munich. Theresa had a son, named Rudolph, from a previous marriage. There was little interaction between Ray and Mary's children and Rudolph, although Diane says, 'Dad paid for Rudolph's education, putting him through college'.[17]

According to Pam, their stepmother was 'a hard-hearted woman'. 'She never accepted Barry and was very unkind to him,' Pam says. 'Thea, as we called her, once hit one of my children, my first-born, Hamish, when he was a toddler, in the presence of Barry. That was the first and only time I've ever seen Barry get really angry. He stood and walked towards her. Dad called out, "Barry! Don't Barry!" And my lovely, gentle big brother took out his frustration by throwing his dinner plate into the sink.

'Anybody who couldn't treat Barry as they would treat me or anybody else didn't figure in my life. My attitude didn't change, even when I started going out with boyfriends. Barry tried with Thea. He really tried.'[18]

Diane says that Barry and Rudolph were never close. One hot summer's day Barry and Rudolph went swimming. Barry got into difficulties in the water and was floundering, but his stepbrother did nothing to help him. Barry has never forgotten the experience, but he is reluctant to talk about it.

But despite the tension of the new family life, Ray Rees remained a 'rock' for his children, especially his son Barry.

Ray Rees had faced pessimism thrown his way by more than one doctor over Barry, whom they considered to have limited life choices.

Family friend Joyce Guthrie recalls: 'Ray was told by a variety of doctors that Barry would never live long enough to reach his teenage years. How wrong they were!'[19]

Michael Woolley, a long-time friend of Barry's, was born with cerebral palsy. Michael is a stalwart of the Sturt Cricket Club and has attended just about every Test and Shield match at the Adelaide Oval for the past 62 years. Michael says: 'My first dealing with Nugget was to hear about him from my mother, who was a cleaner at Colonel Light Gardens School. I heard about this polite youngster who attended the school's opportunity class. Mum would tell me all about this boy who was as mad on the game of cricket and all sport as I was. In attending the opportunity class the children were in the common playground, but there was a certain amount of rejection of those in that class by the rest of the school students. Kids tend to marginalise someone who is different.

'I know that Ray, as all loving parents do, wanted the best for Barry and my mum told me that a teacher at Colonel Light Gardens School, Nancy Bampton, helped Barry a good deal. At that time Barry was getting on famously with everyone— you know Nugget doesn't see an evil bone in anyone he meets. In all the years I've known him, Barry hasn't changed.'[20]

Both Joyce Guthrie and Paula Keily believe that Ray was 'over-protective' of Barry. Joyce says, 'He wrapped him in cottonwool. It was Ray's brother, Bill, who told Ray to "get Barry into sport or something; he'll blossom in something he really likes".'[21]

Barry had no ambitions regarding future employment, although he did occasionally help his father. At the age of 18, he had never experienced a full-time job.

In 1962, Ray was secretary of an accounting firm which worked on behalf of St Peter's College, owner of a building in the centre of Adelaide which was rented to Rowe & Jarman, a retail sports store.

One day Ray Rees went into the store and said to co-owner David Rowe, 'I'm worried about my son, Barry. I need to find something useful and fulfilling for him to do with his time.'

'Ray was unusually concerned,' David recalls. 'He asked if we could use Barry in a way just to occupy his time. He said not to worry about paying him or anything. Perhaps he could sweep the floor, or something. I told Ray, "We'll find something."

'I interviewed Barry. And he didn't say a word. He just sat and looked at me and said nothing. I told him he had the job and I went to my partner and said, "Jar, I'm not sure about what I have done here, but I've given young Barry Rees a job."

'Jar just said, "Don't worry Tidd. It'll be okay. He'll be fine."'[22]

Barry Rees began at Rowe & Jarman in the summer of 1962–63. Barry Jarman recalls the day he first set eyes on Barry Rees: 'He sat in a chair opposite me and shifted nervously in his chair. "Who's your favourite cricketer, Barry?" I asked him.

'He responded immediately. "Keith Miller, Mr Jarman."

'I said, "Okay, then, Barry, from now on you are to be called Nugget, after the great Keith "Nugget" Miller.'[23]

And so Barry Rees became Nugget.

On Nugget's first day, Barry Jarman led him to a quiet area of the store where Nugget was given his first task. Jarman took a feather-duster and showed Nugget how he wanted him to dust a stack of tennis racquets.

Barry recalls: 'Nugget didn't say much. He just nodded and began to dust a racquet. I walked off and was doing something in the basement when someone walked into the shop and I came up to serve him. The customer said, "Who's that bloke upstairs cleaning the tennis racquet?"

'I raced upstairs and found Nugget hanging on to the same racquet he started with and there were feathers all over the floor.'[24]

In cleaning the racquet, Nugget had worn all the feathers off the duster until only the stick was left. Barry Jarman spoke gently to him: 'Now mate, here's another feather-duster. Clean one like this and then the next...' Fortunately, Barry says, 'Nugget caught on straightaway and from that moment on he went from strength to strength.'[25]

The monotony of such tasks was never going to raise Nugget's skills, as Barry Jarman was well aware, and he decided that the young man might become a good messenger boy. So he sent him out on a message.

Three weeks later Nugget's father turned up at the store. He wanted to take his son home early. When Jarman said that Nugget was out on a message, Ray became worried. 'Oh, no, no. Barry mustn't go out on a message. He doesn't understand traffic and the lights and all that sort of stuff.' Ray had spoken of his concerns about his son in traffic to David Rowe when he first asked if Nugget could be given some sort of employment, but David hadn't told his business partner.

Jarman explained to Ray that, in fact, Nugget had been delivering lots of messages, every day for the past three weeks. He recalls that 'Ray just stood there and stared at me. He was dumbfounded.'[26]

On Thursday, December 7, 1962, Barry Jarman introduced Nugget to the South Australian cricket team. The players were training at Adelaide Oval before a Sheffield Shield match and Nugget went with Barry to the ground to meet the players and to watch them practise. Suddenly Nugget found himself in the company of his State cricket heroes: Les Favell, Garry Sobers, Ian Chappell, Neil Hawke, Ken Cunningham and, of course, Mr Jarman.

All the players took an instant liking to Nugget and Favell invited him to have a bat against the players. 'Okay, Nugget, let's have a look at your batting. Put the pads on.'

What an opportunity! Nugget's heart pounded and he had Neil Hawke's pads on in a flash. He also borrowed Ian Chappell's gloves and Garry Sobers' bat.

Sobers opened the bowling and Nugget cut and drove with majestic power. In no time at all, Nugget was on 99. But then he lost his middle stump when a ball from Sobers curled in late. He was yorked. Nugget was devastated at being bowled for 99 in his first big innings. Fortunately, though, a no-ball was called and Nugget survived to get that vital one more run.

When Ray Rees collected Nugget from Adelaide Oval that day, Nugget enthusiastically took his dad through the joy of batting against his heroes. 'Dad, I've just scored my first hundred!'

It was the beginning of Nugget's long and distinguished career at the crease.

Barry Jarman took Nugget to all four days of the Shield game and he was allowed to sit in the players' viewing area in the George Giffen Stand. Not only had Nugget hit a century against his heroes, but here he was rubbing shoulders with them at the ground during the match.

At the end of play on the first day, the two teams settled down together to have a beer and talk over the game. Nugget sat next to Mr Jarman and hardly said a word. But he watched and he listened and he learnt. He met Richie Benaud, Norm O'Neill, Alan Davidson and Johnny Martin. Nugget's involvement with the Australian cricketers had begun.

The cricket season was well underway and Barry Jarman believed there might be a role for Nugget, delivering messages from the State and Test players to his retail sports store—a player might want a new handle on his bat, a new pair of batting gloves, a protector.

The players instinctively and immediately warmed to Nugget. He was efficient and prompt with his messages. Nugget would take tickets to the gate for the players. He quickly got to know all the attendants and gatekeepers, even the people manning the hotdog stand which stood on the western asphalt terracing of Adelaide Oval.

Sometimes a player would slip Nugget a note, asking him to give the message to the pretty blonde sitting near the players' gate on the edge of the ground. While the players watched Nugget performing his errand from the home dressing-room, a team member (invariably Neil Hawke) might put field-glasses to his eyes and, with the most painfully sarcastic English accent, would give a commentary:

'Ah, now here comes the portly Nugget Rees, looking for all the world like a young version of that other elongated pear, Colin Cowdrey. He has stopped near the gate and fumbles for the written note in his pocket. With the note in his left hand, he taps the pretty blonde girl gently on the right shoulder. Nugget is now bowing, as if addressing royalty. He is shaking hands. She is laughing, Nugget is smiling and continuing to shake the girl's hand. He backs off, salutes, then gives her the thumbs up.'

The girl opens the note and turns her head, looking up at the players in the viewing area. She smiles. Nugget's job is done. His head is down, his arms at his side as he marches back towards the dressing-room. As he comes past the players' area, someone yells, 'Nice girl, eh Nug? Big jugs, eh Nug?'

Nugget chuckles. 'A very nice girl. Nice girl,' Nugget says, but he will not enter into any banter which would offend. Nugget is a true gentleman.

That first season with the State side was also the beginning of another tradition which continues to this day—Barry Jarman took Nugget on tour with the SA team. But first Jarman needed to clear the idea with the skipper, Les Favell.

Barry recalls: 'Favelli said, "Who'd—you know—look after him?"

'"Well," I said. "I'll do it. He can stay in my room with me."

'Favelli agreed, so too Nugget's father, who paid the fares and accommodation. From that time on Nugget toured every year with the SA team.

'That first time in Melbourne, Nugget proved to be the tidiest bloke of them all. He even made his own bed. I said to Nugget, "Now mate, you are living here in a hotel, you don't have to make your own bed."

'He looked me squarely in the eye and said, "Mr Jarman, I've been taught to treat other people's homes as my own and I always make my own bed at home."

'Everything in the room was perfectly tidy—except the bathroom. After Nugget had showered, I walked into the room and it was thick with Johnson's Baby Powder.'[27]

Even in those early cricket days with the State side, Jarman had already begun to see the special characteristics of this remarkable young man. Nugget's manners were impeccable, he knew, but he didn't realise to what extent Nugget took his chivalry. He recalls one particular occasion: 'We were on tour in Brisbane and a few of the players were sitting around a table. The waitress came to our table and Nugget stood up and I asked, "What are you standing up for, Nugget?"

'He replied, "I always stand up when a lady comes to the table."

'We all learnt something that night.'[28]

Back at Rowe & Jarman, Nugget's work was going well but Barry Jarman noticed that it was gradually taking him longer to complete his round of messages. 'Nugget got to know everyone, especially the small dealers in Adelaide, the engravers, the bookmakers, the watchmakers, all those hands-on small business people,' Jarman says. 'He knew them all, every single one of them—Nugget became a household name in the city. But he got slower with his messages because he'd stop in every shop, race in and say, "G'day Jack, G'day Bill".'[29]

David Rowe discovered that Nugget believed implicitly in 'same day service': 'Nugget would go to the bootmakers or the watch repair shop. He got to know them all pretty quickly and they got to know him and gain such affection for him. But Nugget refused to leave their shop until he had Mr Jarman's watch repaired or Wally Grout's boots fixed. He simply waited until they got the job done. And because they loved him, they repaired the item straightaway.'[30]

A youngster named Bob 'Swan' Richards, who was just twelve years old when he began with Rowe & Jarman in the same year as Nugget, used to get the lunches for the staff, but Swan was always getting the orders and money messed up. So Barry Jarman and David Rowe decided to give the job to Nugget.

In this, as in everything he did, Nugget was methodical. Jarman recalls: 'One day, just as Nugget was about to leave the store to get the lunches, I yelled out, "Hey, Nugget, how about getting me a pie?"

'I was surprised when he said, "Oh no Mr Jarman, I'll do it when I come back."

'"No mate. Get the pie with all the other orders."

'"No, I can't, Mr Jarman. I'll do it when I get back."

'It was really unusual for him to refuse and he seemed a bit agitated, so I decided to follow him.

'He walked into the deli and the bloke behind the counter beamed and started talking about Port Adelaide or something. Nugget reached into his top pocket and took out a piece of paper. The money was inside. Mr Rowe's order, a pie and a Coke.

'With each order, Nugget would get the change and wrap it in the note and place it in one of his pockets. He had a separate pocket for each one. That was why he couldn't get my order. He only had enough pockets to cover the four orders. Clever. Nugget, very clever.'[31]

Jarman knew then why Nugget never messed up a lunch order—not one mistake in thousands of lunches over 25 years.

Notes

1   Pam Freeman to author, April 2008
2   ibid.
3   ibid.
4   ibid.
5   ibid.
6   ibid.
7   Ron Mitchell to author, April 2008
8   Pam Freeman to author, April 2008
9   ibid.
10   ibid.
11   Paula Keily to author, April 2008
12   Joyce Guthrie to author, April 2008
13   Diane Smith to author, August 2007
14   Extract from Woodville District High School, 'Summary of School Record of Raymond G. Rees', Di Smith's personal papers
15   Di Smith to author, August 2007
16   Pam Freeman to author, April 2008
17   Di Smith to author, August 2007
18   Pam Freeman to author, April 2008
19   Joyce Guthrie to author, April 2008
20   Michael Woolley to author, December 2007
21   Joyce Guthrie to author, April 2008
22   David Rowe to author, April 2008
23   Barry Jarman to author, June 2007
24   ibid.
25   ibid.
26   ibid.
27   ibid.
28   ibid.
29   ibid.
30   David Rowe to author, April 2008
31   Barry Jarman to author, June 2007

CHAPTER 3

Nugget's new world

When Nugget began working at Rowe & Jarman, a whole new world was opened to him.

On his first day Nugget said little, but he watched and he listened. Late that Tuesday afternoon he met Russell Moyle, who ran the workshop and was expert in effecting all manner of sporting goods repairs, from tennis racquet re-strings to broken cricket bats, hockey sticks and footballs. Russell approached the painfully shy newcomer and shook his hand—it was the beginning of a lifelong friendship.

Because Barry Jarman and David Rowe were constantly on the move and interacting with customers upstairs, Nugget found himself in the workshop on a regular basis and Russell became Nugget's mentor. Russell would talk to Nugget while he worked at his benchtop. He taught Nugget about money, spreading various denominations of coins on the table and asking Nugget to build a stack amounting to $1.50. And he taught Nugget how to negotiate traffic in the city—when to walk, on green, and when to stop, on red.

He also taught him how to tell the time. Even though Nugget had worn a watch for most of his teenage years, he couldn't read it. Every time Nugget came through to the workshop, Russell would look up from his bench and say, 'Nugget, what's the time please?' Then came the day when Nugget's face beamed and he answered politely: 'Russell, the time is five minutes past eleven, thank you very much.'[1]

Russell soon learnt that whenever he told Nugget anything, Nugget caught on immediately. He never forgot a face, a name, a piece of advice or an instruction, and Russell never had to repeat himself.

It didn't take long for all the staff at Rowe & Jarman to discover that Nugget had the most remarkable memory. They learnt to rely on Nugget to remind them about a dental or doctor's appointment. A couple of days before the due date, Nugget would sidle up to someone and say, 'Don't forget your appointment on Friday'.

Storeman Arthur 'Slugger' Slee, who was at the store the day Nugget began, recalls: 'I remember Tidd giving him a cloth and asking Nug to wipe the dust off the golf clubs. We had the clubs in a pretty crude wire rack. I came back to see how he was going and he was still wiping the same three-iron he started on.'[2]

Slugger, so named by David Rowe after having watched him play golf, often drove Nugget home on Friday nights and remembers Nugget's fantastic memory: 'Even at the dead of night, Nugget always knew the way home. He directed and I drove. Never failed.'[3]

He was also impressed by Nugget's 'lovely manners'. He says, 'Nugget gave everyone at the store a present every Christmas. He gave chocolates to the office girls and a little gift to others. The great thing was that Nugget's giving was genuine. It came from his heart.'[4]

David Rowe's son, Mike, began work at the shop as a youngster running messages with Nugget. Mike often relates how Nugget and he would stand in a shop for a very long time before they were served, because Nugget politely allowed everyone in the shop and those who came into the shop to be served first. Nugget believes to this day that allowing people to the front of the line is 'the right thing to do'.

But it was Russell Moyle who, perhaps more than anyone there, began to notice more special things about Nugget. He found Nugget to be extraordinarily perceptive. 'Nugget "picked" a person better than anyone I've met,' Russell says. Russell's brother-in-law, Paul, was a sports marketer, and a Sydney-based work colleague of his visited Adelaide with the intention of selling a lot of his product there. While on a message, Nugget met the man briefly in the street. When Nugget returned to the shop, he wore a concerned look.

'Nugget said to me, "Russell that man is no good. I tell ya, he's no good, no good at all, Russell." And almost six months to the day Nugget spoke with him that bloke was jailed for fraud.'[5]

When the ABC's Wendy Page speaks of Nugget as 'part-Rain Man, part-Forest Gump' she refers to Nugget's child-like Forest Gump 'take' on the world and the Rain Man genius within. Nugget was a bit slow on one hand, but on the other he possessed great sensitivity and perception.

Nugget lived for cricket in summer and football in winter. At work he couldn't have wished for a better environment. In the workshop he learnt from Russell Moyle, and he also had a great relationship with Arthur Slee. There was always banter and Nugget soon learnt to give as well as receive. He became adept at one-liners and when someone had a light-hearted 'go' at Nugget, he came back confidently with a clever little quip. And with his reply there was his trademark broad grin and the double thumbs up.

Rowe & Jarman became an icon of South Australian business. People loved the quality of the service as much as the quality of the goods. Among the staff were State golfer Cathy Anderson (who married store manager Geoff Barton), Jane Usher, Marg Muzurke, Marie Gray, Jan Schulz, and Fay Gulliver and Wendy Robbins, who had both worked in the office for more than 20 years. The girls loved Nugget's daily greeting—'Hello dear, how are you? How are the kids?'—and their Christmas box of chocolates.

Nugget also enjoyed rubbing shoulders with blokes such as John Saunders, West Torrens footballer David Raggatt, Glenelg cricketer and baseballer John Papandrea, Russell Moyle's son, Phil, who helped his dad in the workshop, and fishing expert Don Webster. Others included Don Tessesrie, North Adelaide footballer Brenton 'Snake' Anderson, computer man Steve Goldsmith, Glenelg, Essendon and Norwood footballer Paul Weston, and Port Adelaide footballers Alan Greer and Neville 'Chicken' Hayes.

Russell Moyle says that in those days Rowe & Jarman was 'a magic place to work'.

'BJ [Barry Jarman] and Tidd [David Rowe] were terrific bosses. There was a great environment in the shop. And they simply loved Nugget.'[6]

Barry Jarman is a sporting icon—Australian Test player, selector, administrator, international match referee, racehorse owner and TV commentator, Jarman has done it all and in 1997 he was awarded the Order of Australia (OAM) for service to sport.

Jarman's grandfather, Fred May, was a huge influence on Jarman's early sporting life. Jarman says: 'He once captained a South Australian country 18 cricket side against Andrew Stoddart's England team in 1897–98. And he played centre-half-forward for South Adelaide, and was said to have been the first footballer to kick a goal from a set shot, other than a place kick.'[7]

Jarman recalls that Fred used to sit in the same seat in the George Giffen Stand at Adelaide Oval, watching every game of cricket and football he could for more than 40 years. 'And often as a boy I would accompany him, and I dreamed of emulating my cricket and league football heroes.'[8]

'Of course I had an ambition to wear an Australian cap,' Jarman says—an ambition he later achieved, as the Australian cricket team's wicket-keeper. Jarman played 19 Tests for Australia between 1959 and 1969, scoring 400 runs at 14.81 with a highest score of 78. He took 50 catches and stumped four batsmen. In 191 first-class matches Jarman scored 5615 runs at 22.73, with five centuries—his highest 196. He took 431 catches and 129 stumpings.

Jarman toured South Africa (1957–58); India and Pakistan (1959–60); New Zealand twice (1956–57 and 1966–67); and England three times (1961, 1964 and 1968). He was also vice-captain to Bill Lawry in 1968, and when Lawry was injured he led the side for his only match as Test captain in the Leeds Fourth Test.

Never a man to hold back when he saw injustice, Jarman, as an International Cricket Conference (ICC) match referee, confiscated a ball from the South African team during a one-day international against India in 1997 because he believed the ball had been tampered with by the Protea bowlers. Jarman noticed that after 16 overs had been bowled, the ball suddenly began to swing all over the place. He took immediate action, instructing the umpires to replace the ball, much to the displeasure of Bob Woolmer who was the South African coach at the time. Jarman says, 'Later, two South African players came up to my hotel room and apologised.'[9]

As an ICC referee, Jarman became good friends with former South African captain and administrator Peter Van der Merwve, who, after being introduced to Nugget, always asks after him. 'Peter would phone me, still does, quite frequently and his final words are always, "And how is Nugget going?"'[10]

Like Barry Jarman, David Rowe also made his name in sport, but Rowe did so on the tennis court. 'Tennis was a family passion,' Rowe explains.[11] Born in Adelaide, Rowe is the son of Ernie Rowe, who won the South Australian Tennis Championship in 1926–27 and represented Australia in an international against France in 1930. He also wrote two books on tennis. Rowe's grandmother, Florence, or Flo, was married to Walter Tidd Rowe and she won the State titles.

Rowe says, 'I had a state ranking of six (I made a good practise partner) and with Don Candy, Ken McGregor and Dudley Goodger we won the Linton Cup for South Australia in 1947.'[12] They were to celebrate the 60th anniversary of their win but sadly Ken McGregor died in December 2007.

When Rowe thinks back through his tennis-playing days, there's one incident he'll never forget: 'In the early 1950s I played centre court against Ken Rosewall on day one of the South Australian Singles Championship. Some 6000 people turned up, no doubt because a week earlier Ken and Lew

Hoad wrested the Davis Cup from the Americans. Ken won the first set 6–4, then the referee came out and said to me, "Don't know you can handle this—you are not allowed to leave the arena—but you have played that set with your fly undone!"'[13]

Golf was also a family passion and when Ernie Rowe was 86 years old he shot 80 off the stick. Rowe is glad his father made him a junior member of Kooyonga Golf Club when he was a teenager as Kooyonga has become 'a second home'. David has been president and captain of Kooyonga. He played pennant golf, and at his best he played off a handicap of 6. As he nears 80 years of age, he still manages to play to a handicap of 14.

David Rowe and Barry Jarman worked together at D.V. Thomas Sports before they decided to start up on their own. Rowe says, 'I wanted the store to be called Jarman & Rowe, but Jar was adamant that it had to be Rowe & Jarman. We tossed a coin and Jar won the toss.

'In 1960 we got a little place in Twin Street, Adelaide. It was very small. My dad put up his home as security with the bank to give Rowe & Jarman some capital. I borrowed £100 from my wife Betty as a float to put in the till. She often says at an appropriate time, "When do I get my £100 back?" The shop fixtures were tea chests, but we did put a net up to practise our golf.'[14]

* * *

If every day was a joy working at Rowe & Jarman, Nugget's weekends were filled with sport, football or cricket. Nugget enjoyed the success of the Port Adelaide Magpies. He had watched the Magpies from an early age, going to Alberton Oval with his dad Ray and his uncle Bill. He had watched all the great players, and premiership flags seemed to roll out of Alberton like a production line. Fos Williams began the great and unrelenting tradition of winning (he coached the Magpies to seven flags, including one golden period of six successive premierships); Jack Cahill coached Port to an extraordinary ten premierships; and in recent seasons Steven Williams (Mark Williams' brother) got a couple. On cold days Nugget would wear the Port Magpies colours in the shop; a scarf or a beanie, or both.

Just seven days after US President John Kennedy was assassinated in Dallas, Nugget saw SA beat WA by an innings and 102 runs in the match which began on November 29, 1963. One of Nugget's mates, SA captain Les Favell, hit 141. That same summer the South Africans belted Australia at Adelaide Oval, with 18-year-old Graeme Pollock hitting 175 and Eddie Barlow, 201. Another Nugget favourite, Neil Hawke, took 6/139 in 39 overs of clever swing bowling.

A few months later, Barry Jarman left for England with the 1964 Australian cricket team. In England, Jarman and Norm O'Neill exchanged their Test caps. Jarman says, 'When Normie and I toured together we always swapped caps for his fitted me perfectly and vice-versa.'[15] When Jarman got back from England, he presented Nugget with the cap. Inside bears the name 'N.C. O'Neill'. Nugget was delighted.

In the summer of 1964–65 Doug Walters hit a career-best 263 for NSW against SA. He then took 7/63 to complete a wonderful all-round effort. Walters had little trouble with the SA batsman, but later in the return match against SA at the SCG, Walters came up against a very determined Nugget Rees. It was after stumps on day one of the game. Walters was bowling and Nugget hit a brilliant 145 before Walters finally got his man, caught behind by Brian Taber. That epic knock was even more significant for Nugget because it was the first time he wore the baggy-green cap of Australia.

Then in the summer of 1967–68, Nugget got to wear his baggy-green cap in the presence of Barry Jarman and the rest of Bob Simpson's Australian team. Australia was playing India and Jarman, who had long played in the shadow of Queensland wicket-keeper Wally Grout, had become the regular gloveman. Nugget was in his element. Mr Jarman was in the Test squad and Nugget was there among his heroes wearing the baggy-green.

Barry Jarman played his last Test for Australia against the West Indies at Adelaide Oval in 1968–69, but he played the rest of the summer with SA, and Les Favell's team won the coveted Sheffield Shield. Les Favell retired a year later and he handed the captaincy to Ian Chappell. He also handed the baton of the Nugget tradition to Chappell.

That summer, South African great, Barry Richards, scored runs in Bradman-like fashion, hitting 1500 runs at an average of 115. Nugget was now sitting alongside Richards among a number of new faces. Favell and Jarman had retired, but Nugget always made it his business to learn all he could about the new players. He often knew their club match statistics better than them. He welcomed each man into the fold.

In the early 1970s in Adelaide, Nugget was perhaps the most recognisable face in the central business district.

But his fame crept up on David Rowe and Barry Jarman. David Rowe believes that they weren't seeing what others were seeing. 'I guess we didn't realise the extraordinary development in Nugget that other people were increasingly noticing,' he says.[16]

But the realisation hit David when Nugget took on the task of banking maintenance money for the store manager, Geoff Barton, affectionately known as 'Bart'. David says: 'Nugget's role was to bank the money Bart had collected for him. Nug soon realised what day the maintenance was due and he would say to Geoff in a loud voice in front of everyone in the store, "It's maintenance day, Mr Bart. Got your maintenance money ready?"'[17]

The time came when David Rowe felt Nugget needed a higher profile at the shop. It was decided to produce and sell Nugget's Bat Oil under the Rowe & Jarman official label.

NUGGET'S BAT OIL

SOLD BY

ROWE & JARMAN

91 GRENFELL STREET, ADELAIDE

38 PLAYFORD AVENUE, WHYALLA

SHOP 10 WESTLANDS, WHYALLA

BOTTLED BY BARRY REES

Nugget's Bat Oil was pure linseed oil. Rowe & Jarman staff always used the sales pitch: 'Beware of substitutes—Nugget's Bat Oil is the real McCoy.' David recalls: 'Nugget used to take great care using a funnel to pour linseed oil from a large can into each medicine bottle, then carefully adhering the special label. Nugget's Bat Oil was very much his "baby".'[18]

Then came the day when Nugget's Bat Oil received more fanfare than usual. Usually, the order placed to the Faulding Company was for a half a gross of the glass bottles. In was storeman Arthur 'Slugger' Slee's job to order the bottles but one day he was away sick so Nugget was asked to ring the Fauldings Company to place Rowe & Jarman's order. Instead of half a gross of bottles, Nugget ordered twelve dozen gross: 20,736 bottles!

Barry Jarman recalls: 'A big semi-trailer turned up at the corner of Chesser and Grenfell streets, stopping traffic in all directions. There were pallets of the bottles.'[19]

Nugget's Bat Oil proved extraordinarily popular, evidenced by the fact that not one of the original bottles appears to have survived. (Rob 'Super' Elliott, however, did keep one of the original Nugget labels.)

Former Port Adelaide Magpies footballer Alan Greer worked at Rowe & Jarman with Nugget. He remembers that one day Nugget was given the job of checking inward goods: 'The Barna table-tennis balls came in a carton and within that carton there were little boxes each containing six balls. When they were packaged up, you simply didn't rip them open to check the number. However, Nugget did do that and he found that one of the boxes had only five table-tennis balls in them—one short!'[20]

Greer left Rowe & Jarman in 1967 to start up a sports goods business in Grote Street with Geof Motley. 'I didn't see a lot of Nugget after that. He'd still come in to see us, but only here and there. However, I have had a good deal to do with Nugget in recent times. I often have a cup of coffee with him at Alberton Oval before having a look at the Power train. Nugget's integrity is A1. When he is your friend, Nugget is your friend for life.'[21]

On another occasion while Nugget was inward goods check clerk, a consignment of golf balls arrived at Rowe & Jarman's store. A truck was parked in Chesser Street and the golf balls, all loose, were in cardboard boxes, each containing a gross of balls. The boxes were loaded onto a platform, like a large dumb waiter, and the platform was hoisted to the first floor landing by a series of pulleys. Nugget was at the opening to the landing when the first box arrived. He picked it up and the bottom gave way.

'I don't think I've ever seen so many golf balls bouncing about,' Jarman says. 'Here we are in the middle of the city at lunchtime. The bouncing golf balls stopped the mid-day traffic for a quarter of an hour.'[22]

In 1963, the Port Adelaide Magpies won their first premiership since their fabulous run of six flags on the trot (1954–59) in which Geof Motley, recently included in the AFL Hall of Fame, was a key member. Geof says: 'I've known Nugget since the early 1950s. He used to turn up to Alberton Oval and there was never a more enthusiastic and encouraging barracker. I'd hear this distinctive voice, "Geoffrey Motley, number 17!" and I didn't even have to turn around. I knew it was Barry Rees.

'Nugget has always called me Geoffrey, never Geof. I don't know why. From that very first time I met him he has been the same and he's always the same next time you meet, the second or 500th time. He doesn't need a gold pass to get into the Port rooms, but he's got a golden knuckle. Nugget only has to knock on the door and he's in. He is the most lovable character.'[23]

Geof Motley worked in the sports goods business, and in the early 1970s he wanted to sell out his share of the company to Russell Ebert. 'But Russell wanted to work with me and he eventually bought Alan Greer's share. Nugget would still pop in and see us. His enthusiasm is remarkable and quite infectious.'[24]

Motley went on to become a manager for a number of AFL players. His son, Peter, was a brilliant footballer who was playing for Carlton when he was seriously injured in a car accident. 'Nugget still keeps in touch with me and with Peter. He is a wonderful human being.'[25]

Russell Ebert, champion Port Adelaide and North Melbourne footballer, and winner of four Magarey Medals—the highest individual award in the SANFL, given to the player who is awarded the most number of 'fairest and best' votes by umpires in a season—has always had the utmost respect and admiration for Nugget. Ebert admits they tried to lure Nugget away from Rowe & Jarman, but 'I'm afraid Nug was always above our salary cap'.

'I got to know and respect Nugget,' Ebert says. 'In those early days there were a number of sports stores about and Nugget just broke the ice in terms of us being able to talk with one another.

'Nugget would come into our shop on Monday mornings. If we had suffered a loss, Nugget would give us an honest appraisal on our performance, which really amounted to piss poor, but not in those words. I found Nugget to be a harsh, but fair judge of performance.

'Nugget brings the best out in people. He often mixes in exalted company, rubbing shoulders with prime ministers and Test cricket captains, meeting the Queen. But Nugget always treats people with respect. He treats everyone the same, with respect and courteousness. He has a rare quality. He always—without exception—leaves you with a smile on your face. Nugget is always interested in you, rather than trying to off-load any burdens of his own. He's genuinely interested in you and your family. The world would be such a better place if there were a few more Nuggets around.'[26]

Integral to Nugget's story is Bob Richards, who, as a 12-year-old boy, began working for Rowe & Jarman. Bob was nicknamed 'Swan' by Barry Jarman. 'He kept getting out for a duck, so I decided to call him Swan and the name stuck,' Jarman recalls.[27]

The young, snowy-haired Bob Richards began his love affair with cricket in the early 1960s. He seemed to 'live' in the sports department of Cox Foys, opposite Myers, in Adelaide. 'One day the bloke in the sports department asked me if I'd like to meet a real Test cricketer, Barry Jarman,' Swan says with a big smile. 'So he sent me to Rowe & Jarman. I met Mr Jarman and I must admit from that day on I must have driven him crazy with my questions about cricket bats. I used to pick one up and try it out with a shadow drive, then another, and another, until I got through the whole rack.'[28]

Bob Richards was among a dozen Year 8 'special class' students at Gepps Cross Primary School. When Barry Jarman returned from the 1961 Australian tour of England, the first of his three England tours with the Test team, he found Swan forever at his side. If Swan wasn't grilling Jarman over the quality and performance of every cricket bat on the rack, he was begging him to visit his school and watch the kids play cricket.

Jarman finally relented. 'I turned up at the Gepps Class Primary School and was immediately struck by all the beautifully maintained cricket gear. I asked where they bought all the stuff. I guess I was thinking, why hadn't the school bought their equipment from Rowe & Jarman? "Oh, no," said the headmaster, "that's not new gear. A youngster in our special class, Bob Richards, looks after all our sports equipment. Bob's a whiz with his hands." I cast an eye over the gear and couldn't believe that it was all second-hand. The equipment was in brilliant condition.'[29]

Rowe & Jarman Sports was then in its infancy, but Jarman saw the value in having a boy like Bob Richards on his team. He talked over this possibility with Richards. 'The only drawback was Bob's age. Swan was barely 12 years old when I approached the headmaster, who was delighted at the job prospect and thought the chance of Bob working with Rowe & Jarman ideal. We had to obtain special dispensation from the Education Department, but with the headmaster's blessing, young Bob Richards was given the all-clear to go to work.'[30]

Swan Richards grabbed the job with both hands. He worked under the guidance of Russell Moyle, learning to string tennis racquets and bind cricket bats. Swan soon became expert in repairing cricket bats. From repairing bats, Swan became famous for building a cricket bat from a block of English willow to the finished product. He made bats for the Test players, including Greg Chappell, and designed the Scoop bat used by the dashing David Hookes and Ian Chappell.

Swan recalls: 'When I started with Rowe & Jarman, Nugget was already there. We must have started almost the same day because I'll never forget his cleaning that Pancho Gonzales tennis racquet. I reckon he took all the paint off the wooden frame and stripped all the feathers on the duster.

'Nugget was quiet, hardly said a word. In those early days some people were a bit cruel, like the other kids were to us in the special class at Gepps Cross Primary School. I know how hard it was for me and I realised how difficult it must have been for Nugget. I was among twelve kids in a special class among 1500 students. The majority of the school kids saw us as "special" or "stupid", but that made me more determined to make good.'[31]

Swan lived with his mother, Joan, and brothers Graham and John, in the northern suburb of Blair Athol, 10 km north of Adelaide. Swan had poor eyesight and he struggled to see the blackboard. In addition to his inability to read information on the blackboard, Swan had 'word-blindness': he was dyslexic. In 2007 Swan underwent radical treatment, having a left eye transplant. He is now waiting for his left eye to heal before he has the right eye done.

Swan is the antithesis of Nugget. While Nugget is quiet and well-mannered, Swan is like a bull in china shop. He is always in a hurry, often bumptious, barging his way in, and he can be abrupt and short with people to the point of rudeness. But, like Nugget, Swan is perceptive and has a good heart.

'As the years wore on, Nugget came out of his shell. He really grew as a human being, gaining confidence and self-esteem. When you give someone a chance in life, self-esteem naturally builds. That also happened to me.

'It is all about giving people a chance in life and Barry Jarman and David Rowe gave Nugget and me a big chance. People underestimated Nugget for he always had a fantastic brain. He has always been shrewd and sharp.

'In the early days BJ [Barry Jarman] was always away playing cricket, so Mr Rowe had more to do with Nugget and me. He was always there for us. Our working environment was brilliant—Russell Moyle, Arthur 'Slugger' Slee, everyone. Working at Rowe & Jarman was such a joy.

'BJ is a very generous person. After the 1961 Australian tour of England he brought back gifts from England for the staff. He gave us gold Dunhill cigarette lighters and cashmere sweaters. And he presented me with a 1961 baggy-green test cap. I spent time with BJ and his family at their Henley Beach home. He was a wonderful influence on me and I will always be grateful for his help and guidance.

'There was no rivalry between Nugget and me. He knew his job and I knew mine. Nugget was terrific in getting the lunches and running messages. I remember he'd get Russell, Slugger and me buttered rock buns for morning tea. There was Russell and Slugger giving Nugget a hard time, but the banter was always good-natured and we all had a good laugh. We always laughed with Nugget.'[32]

At the age of fifteen Swan changed his name by deed poll. He wanted his full name to read Robert Milton Swan Richards: 'But they stuffed it up and officially my surname is a hyphenated one, Swan-Richards.'[33] Swan never bothered to correct it. He is universally known as Swan Richards.

'Nugget would take three hours to go a round of messages. He might have to go to Adelaide Sports Depot, John Mehafeys and other sports stores where we often swapped gear. But Nugget would go to other places.

'Before they moved to the Adelaide Oval, the SACA office was in town and Nugget would wander in to say hello to SACA Secretary Hugh Millard and his deputy Darby Munn. They always loved seeing Nugget, but I think he drove them crazy.

'And on the way back to the store, Nugget would call to someone he knew along the street. No matter how busy they were, everyone knew Nugget and they always stopped to chat with him.'[34]

Dutifully, every Monday morning Nugget would go to see Les Favell at the *Advertiser* building in King William Street. Nugget would buy Les a Coca-Cola one Monday, and the next was Les' turn to shout. They'd talk about cricket in summer and in the winter Nugget and Les would discuss the football teams announced on the radio the night before and the lists which appeared in Friday morning's newspaper. Nugget, of course, championed the cause for Port Adelaide and Les was a Norwood man. The pink-coloured pages of the *Sporting Globe* provided these two cricket and football lovers with more ammunition.

Swan reckons Rowe & Jarman hardly got a stitch of work out of Nugget on Mondays and Fridays. Swan didn't realise then, but Nugget had become the best public relations man in town. His contribution to the sports store was priceless.

One day the tough Port Magpies half-back Neville Hayes, nicknamed 'Chicken' because he was fearless in his attack on the ball, found employment at Rowe & Jarman. 'Nugget was always in Chicken's ear,' Swan says. 'Chicken was the "dirtiest" little footballer I've ever seen, but a terrific fella. Nugget drove him mad.'[35]

Neville Hayes worked for eight years as a salesman for Rowe & Jarman. Now living in Tasmania, he remembers fondly his time with Rowe & Jarman, selling sporting goods to schools in and about the Adelaide area. Hayes says Nugget was 'the greatest personality in the whole place. Nugget was the most reliable workmate. He'd go out on a five-minute message and would come back to the shop some two hours later. He always had a lot of people to talk to along the way.

'I remember the days when in winter we used to take Nugget into Chesser Street for a few kicks and in summer we'd bowl to him. He batted as a kid would bat, imagining himself to be Don Bradman or Ian Chappell or Allan Border. When he scored a century, it was as real to him as if he had just peeled off a ton in an Ashes clash at Lord's.

'Nugget had an incredible memory. I remember Russell Moyle lived in a Trust home and he had to pay his rent in Angas Street. Nugget was there, right beside Russell, a day before the rent was due to remind him about his commitment. He never forgot a name or a face. And he never had a bad word to say about anyone.

'A few years back I was in Adelaide, walking along Grenfell Street, and I heard this distinctive voice, "Chicko! Hello Chicko, how ya going?" He was way over the traffic on the other side of the road, but I knew instinctively the owner of that voice. Nugget always called me "Chicko".

'When he was at Rowe & Jarman Nugget was the best-known personality in town. He was everyone's mate. When I saw *Australian Story* it brought a tear to my eye. I was rapt that here was this man of great goodness being recognised for what he is, a lovely person, everyone's friend.'[36]

Neville and his wife Margaret once had Nugget to dinner at their Medindi home. After dinner Nugget asked if he might read the Hayes' three children a bed-time story. 'Marg and I were amazed at the lack of noise coming from the bedroom. We crept up to the room and peeked in, to see

Nugget sitting at the foot of the bed and our three girls—Nina, 6, Sally, 5, and Kara, 4—all tucked up together, absolutely spellbound as Nugget read to them. They were like little angels, listening intently and hanging onto every word from Nugget. It was a beautiful moment. One to cherish.'[37]

It was Barry Jarman who wisely made Nugget the link between the Rowe & Jarman store and the State and Test cricketers. Neil Hawke might want his boots re-studded; Paul Galloway a new bat-handle grip; John Causby his bat re-bound; or Eric Freeman, a replacement toe cap.

Without exception, over a period of 46 years, Nugget always had the repair or the replacement item back to the player in ample time before the game began next morning. Nugget didn't affect the repair himself, but he co-ordinated events and he made sure that Russell Moyle or another Rowe & Jarman tradesman did the job to his satisfaction and in time for him to complete the trip to Adelaide Oval to hand over the goods.

When Rodney Marsh became the Test wicket-keeper, he got to know Nugget well through having his gloves re-faced. Nugget volunteered to have the gloves fixed and back in time for the start of play next day. Marsh agreed, but was a little worried. They were his only gloves. He asked Nugget to have the gloves back in the dressing-room by 10 a.m. next day. Nugget turned up at 9.55 a.m.

As a Test match bowler for Australia in the 1970s, I couldn't find a decent pair of cricket boots. But I was tied to Puma and was obliged to wear the Puma boot. The sprigs were not of the screw-in variety, so when they wore down too low it meant the entire boot had to be replaced. They were light, however, with a thin nylon sole. After a session in the field a bowler's feet were hot and sore, due to the heat generated by the nylon underfoot and the fact that the nylon sole did not allow the shoes to 'breathe'. At the end of a long day in the field each step was akin to walking on a bed of little nails.

The Adelaide-based Puma representative, Hans Ellenbroek, joined Rowe & Jarman and there began a life-long friendship with Nugget. Hans was with Nugget in the Adelaide store, then Nugget moved to the warehouse in Mile End, and when Rowe & Jarman folded the pair found themselves with Sam Parkinson Marketing. At the time of writing they are still working there.

Nugget was almost driven to distraction travelling between Rowe & Jarman and Adelaide Oval, filling orders from the SA and Test bowlers for inner soles to help protect their feet.

Dennis Lillee and Jeff Thomson had their bowling boots especially handmade by Melbourne-based Hope Sweeney. Whenever Lillee and Thommo were at the MCG, Hope would go to the ground and measure them up for another of his famous pairs of boots. All leather, they were beautifully crafted. He would have the bowlers stand on a large white sheet of paper and he would trace the outline of their foot. From his traced image, Hope made the pair of boots. Both of the fast men swore by Hope Sweeney's craftsmanship. Nugget's ingeniousness shone for he managed to drum up business from these two fast-bowlers whenever they were in Adelaide: 'They still needed boot-laces, inner soles, plastic heel protectors and toe caps, didn't they?'

The year of 1977 brought great change to the world. Elvis Presley died, aged 42. Stephen Spielberg's *Close Encounters of the Third Kind* wowed film audiences; *Star Wars* hit the picture theatres; and World Series Cricket shocked cricket throughout the land. Nugget remained loyal to the Test scene. A few of his SA players had 'defected' to WSC, including rising star David Hookes.

On February 17, 1978, the day before Tasmania's first Sheffield Shield match on home soil, Barry and Gaynor Jarman were picked up at Hobart Airport and were being driven to their hotel at Hobart Casino. Jarman was guest speaker at a dinner to commemorate the historic cricket occasion. 'As we reached the top of a hill, I saw players on the field of the old Hobart ground. There was a game going on. A 44-gallon drum had been placed each end of the wicket and there was a familiar figure with a bat in his hand.

'It was Nugget.

'I yelled to the cabbie, "Stop the car!" And we watched Nugget bat. The big, electronic scoreboard said "Nugget 34 not out". He hit a couple of fours and suddenly he was 99.

There was a loud appeal and Nugget was given out. I can still see Trevor Robertson leading his players off and there was Nugget still at the wicket, shaking his head.

'Apparently he pleaded with the players, telling them that a great injustice had been done and that he had not hit the ball. Nugget's appeal was upheld and he returned to the wicket, getting the single he so desperately needed to notch his hundred.'[38]

Swan Richards maintains that it was Ian Chappell who had the greatest influence on Nugget gaining a love and passion for the game of cricket: 'Chappelli, as you know, has a rough and tough macho style, but he is always more bark than bite. Nugget is lovable, drives you crazy, he's at you like a bull terrier, but he's a lovable character. It was Ian Chappell who got Nugget going with the players.'[39]

But Chappelli refutes that claim. He believes the greatest influence came from Barry Jarman. 'Jar brought Nugget to the game at Adelaide Oval. He's been wonderful in his encouragement of Nugget. My early memory of Nugget was when he first went to Rowe & Jarman. I recall Jar telling me that when Nugget began working there, Ray Rees insisted that he pay Nugget's way. He would give Jar money and Jar would put it in a pay envelop and Nugget would receive his pay packet like everyone else.

'I'd see Nugget in the street and we always stopped for a chat. And everyone going past would know Nugget and they'd greet him. Everyone seemed to know him. Then came the time when Jar said to Nugget's dad, "Ray, I'm going to pay Nugget. He's terrific for Rowe & Jarman and he deserves a wage and I'm paying it from now on."

'That's a lasting memory about Nugget. Also, I can recall always having banter with him about his beloved Port Adelaide. And Nugget never spoke ill of any Port player. He was always full of praise and you could never sway him to another team.'[40]

During Ian Chappell's reign as State and Test captain, Nugget's confidence soared.

For a couple of winters Ian Chappell had his State cricket team play in the SA Basketball Association competition. We played in a lowly grade, but it was all good fun and helped team morale. Nugget was, of course, the team's coach-cum-manager.

One night we were having a beer in a local pub near the basketball centre, which was then near the Wayville Showgrounds on the southern edge of the city. Earlier that night our fiery fast-bowler, Kevin 'Cuan' McCarthy, who allegedly punched an opponent, was benched for the rest of the game.

Nugget had already seen the effect of a punch that evening. He then noticed a bloke in the bar raising his arm threateningly in the direction of Ian Chappell. Nugget wasn't known for his fleetness of foot, but this time Nugget moved like lightning, ensuring that he was between his State and

Test captain and the perceived threat. Nugget grabbed the burly bloke's arm in a vice-like grip and released it only when he was convinced by the players that the threat had passed. Whether the man was attempting to strike Chappell we never established. But the incident showed how protective Nugget felt towards the cricketers and his friends. We learnt that within that gentle and rotund frame lay amazing strength.

Nugget's love toward his fellow human beings manifests itself in many ways. One of his favourite sayings is a line he picked up from David Rowe: 'You are rich indeed if you have friends.'

Chappelli fondly remembers Nugget giving his inspirational talks, and particularly the times Doug Walters fed Nugget mischievous lines, such as 'What about BJ's keeping, Nug? Needs to lift his game, eh?' And Nug would reply, 'Oh, no. Mr Jarman's keeping pretty well. He's alright.'[41]

Kookaburra managing director Rob Elliot remembers walking towards the Australian dressing-room at Adelaide Oval with Test selector Phil 'Pancho' Ridings just before resumption of play on the third day of the Fifth Ashes Test of 1974–75: 'Pancho said, "I wonder what pearls of wisdom Chappelli is delivering to his troops. Let's pop in to the dressing-room." We wandered in, looked into the centre of the dressing-room and there was Nugget standing on top of the table, imploring the players to greater deeds: "C'mon Thomson, lift your game. Lillee's bowling twice as fast!" It was remarkable.'[42]

For years Nugget had remained loyal to Gray-Nicolls, using that company's equipment exclusively, particularly the Scoop bat used by Ian Chappell, and the Double Scoop created by Swan Richards. However, before the start of the 2006–07 season, Nugget did not receive a contract from Gray-Nicolls and Kookaburra swooped. Elliot says: 'We had branched out and were manufacturing bats. Nugget, of course, was ever loyal to Gray-Nicolls, but when, in his own words, he was "dropped off" I approached him and offered him a Kooaburra Sports contract.'[43]

Nugget signed a lengthy Cricket Equipment Agreement (valid August 11, 2006, to August 11, 2020). The agreement makes special dispensation for Nugget to take prescribed drugs for the on-going treatment of his diabetes.

In part, the agreement reads: 'You warrant us that you are free to enter into this Agreement and are not contracted to Gray-Nicolls or committed in any way to any other company, firm or person who would be considered competitive or sell similar products to our Equipment. You also warrant that nothing prevents you from performing your obligations under this Agreement. You agree to keep the Confidential information super secret and confidential.

'You also agree not to disclose any Confidential information to any person and don't tell Greg Smythe [Gray-Nicolls chief] without our prior written consent, other than your unprofessional advisor Hans Ellenbroek [Nugget's great workmate] or as required by law. This agreement may be suspended and/or terminated immediately by us if: (clause b) you commit any act including the "jiggy-jig" on tour which in the reasonable judgement of the Company brings you into public disrepute, contempt, scandal or ridicule, offends public opinion or reflects unfavourably on the Company's reputation.'[44]

Nugget's inspirational speeches live in the memory of former Australian Cricket coach, John Buchanan: 'One of the first impressions of Nugget when I became part of the Australian cricket team was how loved he was by the players and support staff. And that love was reciprocated by this gentle man. He had an almost hallowed presence.

'I think it was because he has been part of the Australia dressing-room for well over 40 years. More importantly, it was because of his loyalty. To Nug, Australian players and teams were the best (possibly eclipsing the mighty Redbacks or even Kensington). The team was his friend and he passionately applauded everything they did and said.

'Nugget, dressed in his Test match regalia, gloved up to muffle the incessant clapping and appealing for wickets when Australia fielded, would often stand on the dressing-room table and implore the players with his words of wisdom. And when he stumbled for a word or a thought, there were plenty on offer for him, which he quickly mimicked to the rousing applause of the team just as they left the rooms for another Nugget-inspired assault!'[45]

Former Test great, India and South Australia coach Greg Chappell recalls the time Nugget roomed on tour with current Australian coach and then SA wicket-keeper Tim Nielsen: 'The SACA paid for Nugget's flights and the boys clubbed in for his expenses. Usually Nugget roomed with Peter McIntyre, but on this occasion Peter wasn't there, so Nug roomed with Tim Nielsen, then our assistant coach.

'The first two days Nugget woke Tim at 5.30 a.m. Nug was awake and excited and he wanted to talk to his "roomy". Tim had to explain to Nug that it wasn't fair to wake him so early as he had a long day ahead of him and he had to be on top of his game, so, in future, he was not to make a noise until Tim woke of his own accord.

'The next day Tim awoke around 7 a.m. He was surprised that Nugget had let him sleep that long so he looked over to see Nug lying "at attention" in his bed, afraid to make a sound. When Tim asked him how long he had been awake, Nug said, "Since 5 a.m." God love him!

'Pound for pound, Nugget is one of the loudest clappers in cricket history. He has rather fleshy hands that he claps in a relaxed and loose way that generates an amazing sound.

'He can also talk for Australia. It is not so bad for the boys who are playing the game for they get regular breaks from the chatter and the ear-wrenching sound of his clapping.

'For the support staff and the reserve players though, it can become a little overwhelming, so the system has developed over the years whereby Nug is "sin-binned" from time to time for his over-enthusiasm. The penalties: 1. He has to wear a pair of batting gloves if he claps too much or too loudly. 2. He has to don a batting helmet for a period of time if he talks too much.

'The length of time for each penalty depends upon how many warnings he has been given. The record in my time as coach was a session and a half with the helmet on and two sessions wearing the gloves. Many of the players were happy to lend their gloves for Nugget to wear during penalty sessions for his warm, fleshy hands were great for breaking in new gloves that could initially be a little tight and stiff.'[46]

David Rowe has overseen Nugget's development all the way: 'Nugget goes to Adelaide Oval for all the matches. He knows all the big name players. He still caddies for me at Kooyonga Golf Club, and he seems to win our prestigious "Caddy of the Year" award every year. He once caddied for Greg Norman; he knows all the big names and they know Nugget.'[47]

During the 2005–06 Ashes series Nugget challenged the England captain, Andrew 'Freddy' Flintoff, to a game of lawn bowls at the Adelaide Bowling Club, just behind the Members' Stand at Adelaide Oval. Nugget was suitably impressed: 'Freddy's a terrific bloke. We had a good game and he enjoyed our match as much as I did.'

Barry Jarman and David 'Tidd' Rowe have seen the amazing transformation of the painfully shy boy who became a national hero. David reflects about the Nugget phenomenon: 'Miracle is a bit of strong term, but the way Nugget has developed, well, it is pretty close to a miracle. One day I turned to Barry and said, "Mmmmn, what have we done here, Jar?"'[48]

Jarman remembers how Nugget's dad, Ray Rees, wanted his son to have a job sweeping the floor and that he was very adamant that 'Barry must never go out of the premises'. Jarman says, 'I can tell you that Nugget was brilliant at running messages and getting lunches, a lot better than he ever was at sweeping the floor.'[49]

With David Rowe and Barry Jarman, Nugget had the very best of bosses in the very best of working environments. It was a fabulous team. Nugget thrived in the atmosphere.

Nugget's confidence and self-esteem had grown to such an extent that even his over-protective father, Ray Rees, decided that his son was capable of mowing the lawns at the family home in Unley Park, and Nugget was given special dispensation from his duties at Rowe & Jarman every Wednesday afternoon to mow the lawns at home.

He had been doing the job for months, then one day things went horribly wrong.

Nugget had finished mowing the lawns and leaned over his machine to ensure the cutters were clean. Unbeknown to him the blades were still revolving and as he pushed against the mower he inadvertently started up the machine. Nugget had his right hand under the machine, in the path of the cutters, and he lost the tip of his right index finger. Blood cascaded and Nugget shook in fear and pain.

He was rushed to hospital, but the doctors were unable to save the top of his finger.

His sister Pam, a nursing sister, helped him through his ordeal. 'Nugget was terrific,' she says. 'As he waited to go into theatre there he was laughing and joking with the hospital staff, extolling the virtues of his beloved Magpies and the South Australian cricket team.'[50]

Nugget made a full recovery, but his lawn-mowing days were over.

The SA Shield team went from last in 1974–75 to winning the Sheffield Shield in 1975–76. Australia also beat the West Indies 5–1 in the Test series.

In 1976, a noted cartoonist penned a caricature of Nugget and he had Test cricketers such as Don Bradman, Ian Chappell and Les Favell, among many others, sign it. That caricature was framed and was once in the possession of Nugget's stepmother, Theresa Rees, but Pam rescued it some years back and it now takes pride of place in her lounge-room.

Nugget had a bittersweet 1975–76. A Sheffield Shield under Ian Chappell's captaincy was followed by an extraordinary loss by Port against Norwood in an epic 1976 SANFL Grand Final.

But as Nugget no doubt told the Magpies, 'Tomorrow is another day'.

Notes

1   Russell Moyle to author, May 2008
2   Arthur Slee to author, June 2008
3   ibid.
4   ibid.
5   Russell Moyle to author, May 2008
6   ibid.
7   Barry Jarman to author, May 2008
8   ibid.
9   ibid.
10 ibid.
11 David Rowe to author, May 2008
12 ibid.
13 ibid.
14 ibid.
15 Barry Jarman to author, June 2007
16 David Rowe to author, May 2008
17 ibid.
18 ibid.
19 Barry Jarman to author, May 2008
20 Alan Greer to author, May 2008
21 ibid.
22 Barry Jarman to author, May 2008
23 Geof Motley to author, May 2008
24 ibid.
25 ibid.
26 Russell Ebert to author, May 2008
27 Barry Jarman to author, July 2007
28 Swan Richards to author, February 2008
29 Barry Jarman to author, September 2007
30 ibid.
31 Swan Richards to author, February 2008
32 ibid.
33 ibid.
34 ibid.
35 ibid.
36 Neville Hayes to author, May 2008
37 ibid.
38 Barry Jarman to author, May 2008
39 Swan Richards to author, February 2008

40 Ian Chappell to author, February 2008
41 ibid.
42 Rob 'Super' Elliot to author, Melbourne, February 2008
43 ibid.
44 Kookaburra contract, signed by managing director Rob Elliot
   and members of the Australian Cricket team
45 John Buchanan to author, February 2008
46 Greg Chappell in email to author, March 2008
47 David Rowe to author, October 2007
48 ibid.
49 Barry Jarman to author, November 2007
50 Pam Freeman to author, March 2008

CHAPTER 4

Nugget meets the Queen

For more than ten years Nugget was heavily involved in greyhound racing. Nugget, his sister Pam and her husband Neil Freeman had a successful racing syndicate which won a total of 124 races from the early 1970s to the early 1980s.

Although he had a long association with the trots, Ray Rees wasn't interested in the dogs. 'Dad once asked if our winnings were going to affect our taxation,' Pam recalls. 'I told him that it wouldn't affect us in the slightest, because we get about 50 cents for a win!'[1]

But Nugget loved Saturday nights with the greyhounds at Angle Park.

One of their favourite dogs was Palmerston Lass, by Venetian Court and out of Cappy's Girl. A slow starter, the fawn bitch was invariably last away at box rise and trailed the field. With more than 200 metres to travel, she'd be at the tail and seemingly had no chance of victory. Her backers would put down their glasses. But magically the dog would then accelerate dramatically and flash past the field down the home straight.

Palmerston Lass became known for her barn-storming finishes, and still holds the record of 45.95 seconds for her 755-metre dash at Strathalbyn. The champion didn't win a race until she was three years old, retiring before her fourth birthday with a string of wins and records to her name. During her star-studded career, Palmerston Lass won 25 races with 18 second placings and 9 thirds.

Once at Angle Park she was pitted against the ace Victorian dog, Satanic Power. Satanic Power's connections went on public record saying that no dog in creation could run down Satanic Power once he led the field. After 500 metres Satanic Power led Palmerston Lass by a massive 12 lengths, but Nugget's favourite came home sensationally to win.

Loved by her owners, Palmerston Lass, like all their racing dogs, lived with the Freemans at their Panorama home. Pam says Palmerston Lass and all the other dogs were part of the family. They were never left outside in the cold, rather they were pampered and were offered a hot water bottle in addition to their blanket. If they wanted to, the dogs slept on the beds. The kids played with them, even on race days.

One night a journalist and photographer turned up to do a story on the champion racer and asked to see her kennel.

'Kennel?' Pam asked. 'She's inside.'

The visitors found Palmerston Lass sprawled out under Nugget's chair in the dining room where he was about to slip her a roast potato from his dinner plate.

As Pam Freeman explained to the journalist, 'Palmerston Lass is family. She lives with us and some nights we take her out for a race.'[2]

One of the most necessary and specialised jobs in dog racing is that of a dog catcher. Pam was earmarked for the crucial role from day one, until she became so heavily pregnant with her first child that someone else had to be entrusted with the job.

Pam recalls: 'Neil said, "Give Barry a go." I was a bit hesitant because Dad told me that once Nugget was bitten by a dog and he was frightened by dogs. But we gave Nugget the chance and he was so thrilled. He had his own lead and loved being involved in that way.

'One of our better dogs, Blue Brew, wanted that lure and would take off as if nothing on earth would prevent her from getting it. While Blue Brew was a champion dog and disciplined to always go after the lure, she was very hard to catch. She was feisty and flighty in the kennel. I always had trouble catching her and putting on the lead. But my brother had no such worries with her. Nugget would go to her kennel, put his hand inside and say,

"C'mon girl" and out she would come straightaway, straight to his arms.'[3]

Like Radiant Robert, the champion trotter in Uncle Wal's stable in Woodville, who was a 'mean bugger' to all but Nugget, the greyhounds trusted Nugget. Animals, like people, sensed Nugget's gentle and caring nature.

On the way to and from Angle Park, Nugget sat in the back of the Freemans' car, cuddling the dogs. Win, lose or draw, the greyhounds were made cosy in the back seat and given a drink. On the occasion one of his dogs didn't win, Nugget would talk softly to it, but sufficiently loud enough for Pam and Neil to hear in the front seat. 'It wasn't your fault,' he would say, 'it was the other dog's fault, cutting you off in the straight. That dog didn't give you a chance. Next time, though, you'll win.' Pam reckons Nugget's philosophy with a losing dog was similar to how he reacts to a Port Adelaide loss: 'It was the other team's fault. Bad umpiring.'[4]

There is a stack of photographs featuring Nugget and one of the champion dogs. The winner, Goodnight Irene, seems to be wearing the biggest grin as her part-owner-cum-catcher Barry 'Nugget' Rees holds her on a tight rein for the camera. He is wearing a long, thick black overcoat and chequered bonnet. Nugget is holding the reins with his left hand and the winner's trophy in his right as he kneels for the photographer.

Fame has never affected Nugget in a negative way. Although he never sought recognition, his fame has grown, steadily, since 1962 when he first began at Rowe & Jarman, and it culminated in February 2007 when *Australian Story* made Nugget Rees a household name.

Nugget hit the social pages of the *Adelaide Advertiser* on March 1, 1965, when a photograph of Nugget and sister, Pam, was published, along with details of Nugget's 21st birthday celebrations at the Hotel Australia. 'Guests at the party included Mr and Mrs E. Guthrie with their son David and daughter Dianne, Mr and Mrs K. Keily and their son John, Mr and Mrs A.S. Douglas, Mr and Mrs H. Maplesden, Mr W.J. Rees, Miss Yvonne Wyatt and Mr David Graves.'[5]

I remember writing a feature in 1974 for the *Hills Gazette*, one of thirteen throw-over-the-fence newspapers within the Messenger Press chain: 'He has the uncanny knack of hailing people through dense crowds in Adelaide during peak hours. The voice is unmistakeable, the hair immaculate; the countenance bursting with laughter.'[6]

In September 1981 Nugget was photographed in the *Sunday Mail* presenting the Mail Junior Cricket Award, a new Slazenger Panther cricket bat, to Mark Henbury, 13, of Largs Bay. The runner-up, Nick Pangiotakopoulos, 14, of Adelaide, was given a Slazenger sports bag for his efforts.

After South Australia's Sheffield Shield victory in the 1981–82 summer, the *Adelaide Advertiser* cartoonist, Atchison, featured Nugget kneeling at his bed, with the caption 'And God bless Hookes, Darling, Phillips, Crowe,

Inverarity, Sleep, Wright, Winter, Sincock, Parkinson, Doman and Vincent.' A little bug in the right-hand corner of the cartoon exclaims, as Nugget would exclaim, 'Tell Yer!'[7]

In 1985 Barry Jarman and David Rowe sold Rowe & Jarman, but Barry and David stayed on as consultants to help the new owners. So too Russell Moyle, Arthur Slee and Nugget.

By this time, Nugget was a legend at Adelaide Oval. When he arrived at the ground, he was swamped by people. Everyone wanted to talk to him. He was as well known as any of the Test stars.

Since he first sat alongside the South Australian team in 1962, Nugget had seen first-hand the evolution of his beloved game of cricket. Nugget was there in 1976–77 when Doug Walters returned to Test cricket to hit 107, and when Gary Cosier and Rodney Marsh incurred the wrath of the crowd for their go-slow batting when Australia looked set for an easy outright win over Pakistan. Ever loyal and protective of the players, when quizzed about the Australian pair's go-slow tactics, Nugget said: 'Oh, no that was alright. They did the right thing. They fought hard to stay in so we wouldn't lose.'

In 1985, Nugget witnessed the changing of the guard.

Ian Chappell, Dennis Lillee, Greg Chappell and Doug Walters had all retired. Only Jeff Thomson toured England in 1985, though he was by then past his sensational best. Ian

Chappell had passed the baton of captaincy to Greg Chappell, then came Kim Hughes and Allan Border, who helped drag a very ordinary side to the top.

A number of tremendous players, such as Hughes, Rodney Hogg, Carl Rackemann, Trevor Hohns, John McGuire, Rod McCurdy, Michael Taylor, Greg Shipperd, Terry Alderman and Tom Hogan, quit the traditional game to play two rebel tours of South Africa. Promising South Australian batsman Michael Haysman also went to South Africa. Most of the 'rebel' Australians were paid $200,000 a season and were required to pay a mandatory ONE CENT in taxation.

By then Bob Hawke, Swan Richards' cricket mate, was the Australian Prime Minister. Prime Minister Hawke became so enraged at our top Australian cricketers playing as rebels in South Africa, thus helping to shore up the Apartheid regime in the republic, he effectively closed the gap in the taxation system. But Kim Hughes' rebels got their truckload of tax-free dollars and Australian cricket slipped in the process.

Due to the number of players who opted to play for the rebel team in South Africa, Allan Border was left with a poor team to represent Australia in England in 1985. England won the series 3–1.

One of Nugget's all-time favourite players, Darren Lehmann, debuted for South Australia at the age of 17 and he scored 55 in his first innings. Nugget was there to see the innings and to spend time with the man he now calls 'Uncle Boof'. Lehmann arrived on the scene in the summer of 1986–87, the summer England won the Ashes Down Under.

Nugget well remembered two youngsters who started at Kensington—Tim May and Tom Moody. May was always at Kensington (the Browns), but Moody, whose father taught at Pembroke School, shifted to Perth and big Tom played all his early representative cricket there. Moody's performances for WA got him in Allan Border's 1989 Australian team for England, while May's top-flight spin-bowling for SA also got him on the tour.

Nugget knew them all, from the coach Bobby Simpson to the captain Allan Border. Among the batsmen were Border, David Boon, Dean Jones, Geoff Marsh, Mark Taylor and Steve Waugh. There was bowling strength with Geoff Lawson, Carl Rackemann, Merv Hughes and Tim May, and the side had a top-notch wicket-keeper in Ian Healy, who would go on to prove himself as the best keeper Australia has produced since the mercurial Don Tallon, the champion gloveman of the 1948 Invincibles team. Mind you, Nugget would take anyone to task were they to suggest that any Australian Test keeper could have been better than 'Mr Jarman'.

In September 1988, Rowe & Jarman moved from its Grenfell Street address across the road to Regent Arcade, where the store could spread its wings over two floors. The huge new store was a far cry from the humble shop where Rowe &

Jarman began in 1960. On Monday, November 28, 1988, a photograph was published of some of the staff standing on the escalator of the new store. In the photo were David Rowe, Ian Frazer, Matt Usher, Paul Weston and, perhaps Rowe & Jarman's most well-known face, Nugget Rees.

Swan Richards had left Rowe & Jarman in 1971. As with Nugget, Swan gained in confidence working in the team environment at the shop. His self-esteem soared. Swan was going places. Barry Jarman and David Rowe were surprised when Swan suddenly announced he was going to visit the USSR en-route to England to play cricket. Nugget was sad to see Swan go, but he was happy to see his friend doing the things that he had told him he wanted to do.

Swan spent months in England and gained invaluable experience working for Gray-Nicolls, the famous bat manufacturer. The company Managing Director, Len Newbery, took Swan under his wing. Swan learnt fast and he then became co-founder of a great sporting organisation, the Crusaders.

It all began over dinner at Melbourne's Windsor Hotel. Swan had the idea of bringing together present and past first-class cricketers to play matches against school players. He found allies in two of Australia's leading cricket administrators, Ray Steele and David Richards.

'I wanted former Australian Test wicket-keeper Ben Barnett [who toured England with Don Bradman's 1938 Australian team] involved. Ben and I had been friends since

1970 when I was working for Len Newbery at Gray-Nicolls in England,' Swan says.[8]

The name Crusaders is derived from the word 'crusade'—a cause. The emblem of the Crusaders depicts a bird, a martlet, which is said to have flown above the green sward of England at the time of the Crusades in the 11th century, and is surrounded by stars, representing each state in Australia.

In the beginning, Swan's crusade was to persuade the powerbrokers of cricket and politics to get involved. Today, he has as its patrons former Australian prime ministers Bob Hawke and John Howard, successful businessman Sir Ron Brierley, famous TV host Michael Parkinson, and writer-producer of stage and song Sir Tim Rice. A galaxy of cricket's star players—including Shane Warne, Merv Hughes, Allan Border, Max Walker, David Hookes, Peter McIntyre, Lance Cairns, Sir Colin Cowdrey, Sir Richard Hadlee, Ian and Greg Chappell, Bruce Edgar, Richard Collinge, Gladstone Small, Malcolm Marshall, Jeremy Coney, John Morrison and, of course, Nugget Rees—have turned out for the Crusaders.

Swan knows Bob Hawke well. 'He has always been very supportive of the Crusaders, ever since the days when he headed the ACTU. When Bob became Prime Minister he used to take a hands-on role in selecting his team for the annual Prime Minister's Eleven match. In fact, Bob and I would sit in the Cabinet Room at Parliament House and I'd help him pick the team.'[9]

It was Prime Minister Hawke's influence which resulted in the Crusaders playing the Royal Household at Windsor Castle in 1989 on their first tour. Each second northern summer since then, Swan has taken his Crusaders team to England.

Swan, like Nugget, had become something of an institution.

In 1988 Swan Richards was talking up his planned Crusaders tour of England, scheduled to take place the following year. He had asked Nugget to join the tour.

But the Rees family had more important concerns at home. Ray Rees was fighting terminal cancer.

Pam, a nurse, cared for their father in his last months at the Rees family home in Grove Avenue, Unley Park. She says, 'Dad loved us all a great deal, but he was old school and he rarely showed open affection. One day as I sat with him, we listened to the radio. I think Ken Cunningham was interviewing Nugget. Dad was so proud of Barry. He was beaming. Then when Nug came in, Dad said, "Well done, Barry. But you talk too much. Now go and wash up for dinner."'[10]

Ray Rees died in July 1988.

For Nugget, Pam and Diane, their world was turned upside-down with the death of their father. He was their rock.

After Ray Rees' death the family hardly saw their stepmother again. Most of the precious family photographs and keepsakes disappeared.

Nugget, who loved his father dearly, was heartbroken and angry with his stepmother. 'She didn't go to my father's funeral. To me that was a disgrace,' he says.

After their father passed away, it was determined that Diane and her husband, Rusty, would look after Nugget. Almost immediately the family had to decide whether Nugget would go on the 1989 Crusaders tour.

Not unlike her father, Diane has always been very protective of Nugget. So it was not an easy decision for Diane and Rusty to make. Who would care for Nugget on the tour?

Swan's mother, Joan Richards, would be the team 'mother' and everyone assured Nugget's relatives that he would be well cared for on the trip. Adelaide accountant John Younger, who would be in England for every match of the tour, would also keep an eye on Nugget.

Nugget well remembers the time: 'Dad planned to go to England with me. He would have wanted me to go on the tour anyway. I know that he wanted that to happen. Di and Rusty urged me to go. Somehow I know that Dad knows I toured England with a cricket team. He knows, alright. Dad's now in a good place and he watches over me.'

Among the 1989 Crusaders were Victorian Cricket Association CEO Ken Jacobs, Victorian leg-spinner Peter McIntyre, former Shield fast-bowler Doug Gott, Singapore Airlines boss John MacKinnon, philanthropist and patron

Sir Ron Brierley, and Senator Michael Baume. The side played 29 matches, all one-day affairs, winning 17, losing six and drawing five games. John MacKinnon describes Nugget's role on tour as 'an ace motivator and inspirational guru'.[11] Swan wrote at the tour's conclusion: 'And then there was Nugget. A legend in his own lifetime. Nugget was our most ardent supporter.'[12]

Nugget's England tour included visits to an extraordinary range of places. He went to Uxbridge, Finchhamstead, Petersfield, Hampshire, Wellington College, Eton College, Blossomfield, Eastote, Urchfont, Wiltshire, Eddington, Surrey, Daventry, Northamptonshire, Burton Court, London, Worcestershire, Bagshot and Tunbridge Wells. As well as Windsor Castle, Nugget visited Arundel Castle, the Duchess of Norfolk's ancestral home, where he was photographed with the great England batsman, Colin Cowdrey. Nugget was also photographed dancing the night away in a London bobby's helmet. And he played against the Cricketers Club of London, scoring a compact and thoroughly efficient century.

Of course, Nugget also visited Lord's—the traditional home of cricket.

While at Lord's, Nugget took the opportunity to walk to the centre and examine the turf of the pitch near the spot at the Members' End—the infamous Lord's 'Ridge'—where Barry Jarman had his finger broken by a rearing delivery from England fast-bowler David Brown in the 1968 Lord's Second Test, a match which marked the 200th Test between

England and Australia. Nugget isn't sure whether he saw the exact spot where Mr Jarman was struck, but he looked over the entire square and took it all in.

He even played a few shadow drives.

That day, Nugget was invited into the Australian dressing-room at Lord's. No-one else in the Crusaders party was allowed into the room. It was sacrosanct. Only Nugget could enter.

He was a bit nervous, given Steve Waugh and tail-ender Geoff Lawson were in the process of turning the Australian innings around. Nugget sat next to Tim May, his Kensington and SA mate. He remembers Tim's first words: 'Nug, I can't believe you are here, in England. It is amazing. Here you are at Lord's, the home of cricket. Nugget, here, in the flesh, at Lord's.'

Nugget was sitting in the same room as those greats who have graced the game—from Victor Trumper to Keith Miller, Jack Gregory to Clarrie Grimmett, Bill O'Reilly to Dennis Lillee, and of course, Don Bradman. While he felt humble, Nugget was also happy for he was surrounded by his friends.

As they watched—and Nugget clapped the loudest—Steve Waugh scored 152 not out, and by the end of the Lord's Test match, he had taken his aggregate tally of runs to 350 without being dismissed. Lawson scored a career-best 74 in the Australian first innings, Terry Alderman took his 100th Test wicket at Lord's, and Allan Border became the first Australian captain to twice win a Test at Lord's.

A highlight of the tour was the Crusaders match against the Royal Household at Windsor Castle. Organising this event was a coup for Swan: he dined out on it for years.

Nugget will never forget meeting Queen Elizabeth II and the Duke of Edinburgh.

As the Royal dogs scampered about the Queen's feet, Nugget extended his right hand: 'Pleased to meet you, Your Majesty.'

'And I am pleased to meet you, Nugget,' she replied.

Instinct told him to follow protocol and Nugget observed a pause before he asked: 'And how are the corgis?'

The Royal Household was in uproar. The Queen smiled. 'As you can see, Nugget, they are very well indeed.'

(In mid-2007, Nugget told me with a concerned look, 'There were two corgis at Windsor Castle that day. I think one has since died.')

When Swan introduced the Duke of Edinburgh to Nugget, they shook hands and Nugget said, 'Pleased to meet you, Mr Duke!'

(Swan has a slightly different 'take' on Nugget's meeting with royalty, but I have included Nugget's version here.)

The match against the Royal Household was a thriller. Not since 1964 had the Queen ventured down from Windsor Castle to the derry fields of Frogmore to watch a Royal Household cricket match.

During a slow piece of play, Swan, who was sitting alongside the Queen and in front of Senator Michael Baume, yelled raucously, 'C'mon you blokes, give 'em a touch up!'

The Queen raised her eyebrows. She turned to Senator Baume and whispered, 'Did Swan say what I thought he said—give 'em a touch up?'

'Yes, ma'am, but that's Swan,' the Senator replied diplomatically. 'It is a Swanism, or Swan-lami talk as we say. We don't worry about it.'

'Give 'em a touch up means something quite different in this country,' observed the Queen.[13]

The night before the match, Swan watched a television documentary on the Royal Family. There was footage of the young princesses Elizabeth and Margaret, along with King George V, and other members of the Royal Family.

'I saw you last night, Your Majesty,' Swan said.

'How did you see me last night, Swan?' asked the Queen.

'The documentary about your family, on telly. You were only a tiny tot.'

The Royal Page, John Taylor, interjected on behalf of the Queen. 'Hey, Swan, you can't say that. You can't call the Queen of England a tiny tot.'

'Well, John, in my language she was only a little kid, a tiny tot.'

'Yes, John,' laughed the Queen. 'Swan is right, I was a tiny tot.'

'They all smoked a lot,' Swan said.

'Yes,' agreed the Queen. 'My grandfather [King George V] was a shocker. They all smoked like chimneys.'[14]

In a seat behind the Queen and Swan, Nugget was taking it all in. He wore his Crusaders blazer and trademark broad smile. Every now and then he would clap a good shot. Nugget was in his element, touring England with a cricket team, enjoying the cricket, and especially enjoying his day in the company of royalty.

If only his dad could see him now.

The Queen and the Duke enjoyed the Crusaders' company. They particularly were taken with Swan's unusual command of the English language, and when Swan introduced his captain to the Royal Page, John Taylor, his words brought the house down. 'This is John Page, the Royal Tailor!'[15]

The Queen could hardly contain her mirth.

The Royal Household innings began well with an opening stand of 92, before Swan struck, getting both opening batsmen. However, it was New Zealand-born and Sydney-based corporate giant Sir Ron Brierley's eighth delivery which had the crowd buzzing and Nugget clapping furiously.

The Crusaders' patron delighted all with a high-tossed leggie which he delivered from two paces back from the popping crease. This slow delivery perplexed the batsman Terry Cox—it bounced four times and on each occasion Cox swished and missed badly as the ball bounced along its inevitable way towards the wicket. The ball threatened to bounce a fifth time when it nestled neatly at the base of middle and off-stumps, with just enough force to dislodge the off bail.

Ted Jackson, who was video-taping the match, said it was impossible to view Sir Ron's delivery in slow motion because it would cause the film to stop completely. Former New Zealand batsman Brian Hastings wasn't surprised to learn of Sir Ron's successful four-bouncer at Windsor Castle, for six years earlier, Hastings, playing for Midland St Patricks Cricket Club against Wellington Old Scholars, was clean-bowled by a slow, highly tossed Brierley leg-break which bounced three times before it evaded Hastings' bat and broke the wicket.

The significance of Sir Ron's now famous eighth ball was that it signalled a dramatic collapse of the Royal Household Eleven as both Paul Quinn and Doug Gott picked up valuable wickets. And what did Nugget think of Sir Ron's bowling? 'Very good. Good flight, a bit of spin, and Sir Ron is a very good man.'

A sad time on the tour was the sudden death of one of the members of the Crusaders party, Bob Hooper. Nugget was Bob's Anugraha Hotel room-mate. While watching a game of polo—after Nugget and fellow tour-member Peter McIntyre had befriended two girl polo players—Bob told Nugget and Swan that the trip was magnificent and his life had been fulfilled. He could die happy. As it turned out, he died less than a week later. 'It was terrible,' Nugget says. 'Poor Bob. He was a lovely man.'

Despite the tragedy, the tour pressed on because Bob's widow, Airlie Hooper, was adamant that Bob would not have wanted it any other way.

Swan's mother, Joan Richards, who was the cleaner at Rowe & Jarman for 25 years, was the 'tour mother'. Joan looked after five children on the tour, and, of course, she kept an eye on Nugget Rees.

Most of the time, things ran smoothly for Joan and she was able to live up to her promise to Nugget's sister Diane that Nugget would be well cared for. Except maybe once.

'The night at the hotel in Windsor, I made sure Nugget left the bar at 11 p.m. and saw that he was tucked up in bed for the night,' Joan recalls. 'Next morning at breakfast I said to Swan, "Nugget was good last night. I got him to bed by eleven and later I checked on him and there he was all tucked up in bed, fast asleep." Swan looked at me strangely and said, "Is that right, Mum? Well, how come he was in the bar drinking with us until 1.30 in the morning?"'[16]

On another occasion, during the Crusaders match at Windsor, the Royal policeman at the castle, Stan Highmore, ambushed the Crusaders and escorted them to a pub where they were required to 'drink heartily' lest they be arrested and thrown into jail. The Crusaders, Nugget included, did not argue.

Nugget, aged two, with his Mum, Mary,
and a year later with Dad, Ray

Before they gave Nugget a cricket bat

A five-year-old dressed to kill

At seven, Wild West style,
with sister Pam

Film-star looks at ten

The complete footballer in his Port Adelaide gear, with sisters Pam, left, and Diane

In the front yard at fourteen

A lovely couple. At twenty-one and off to the ball with his sister Pam

An inventive way of walking the family dog!

Celebrating, far right, with the 1975-76 South Australian Sheffield Shield winners.
Far left, a youthful Ashley Mallett enjoys the moment with Terry Jenner, Ian
Chappell, centre, a beer, and in the back row a young David Hookes smiles happily

Every picture tells a story: Bobby Simpson, Ian Healy, the sadly late David Hookes, Darren 'Uncle Boof' Lehmann, Adam Gilchrist, Brett Lee, Glenn McGrath and Ricky Ponting, just a few of the top cricketers, across the generations, with deep affection for Nugget

With some of his favourite Port Adelaide players. From left, Darren Mead, Nick Stevens and Josh Francou

A gear swap with with former Port Adelaide player Stuart Dew – that's Stuart's 2004 Port Power premiership shirt

It's all smiles from Mark Taylor's team after Mark Waugh's brilliant century thwarted a South African victory in the Third Test, Adelaide Oval, February, 1998. It's a bit of a stretch to get an arm around Paul Reiffel!

Flown specially to Sydney for Steve Waugh's swansong Test in 2004, Nugget was included in the final team photograph under Waugh's leadership

As Swan Richards introduces The Queen to the Crusaders at Windsor Castle, behind them Nugget announces himself to The Duke of Edinburgh, 'Pleased to meet you, Mr Duke!'

Time for a glass of wine: toasting Nugget's nephew Hamish Freeman's degree, and relaxing during the Crusaders' 1989 tour of England

Family and friends are everything to Nugget. With sister Diane, left, and Paula and Keith Keily

At an almost Bradman-like ninety-four not out, great friend and neighbour, Phyllis Golding, knows how to behave in front of a camera. With the book written, it's good to see Nugget still smiling with the author!

Captain Nugget at the helm of *Gooda's Gold* , 'Mr Jarman's' houseboat

'Blue Brew' has the biggest smile after winning a race for Nugget and co-owners, brother-in-law Neil Freeman and his wife Pam, Nugget's sister

A happy evening with Wendy Page, Producer of the outstanding *Australian Story* on Nugget, 'Man of the Century'. Wendy is holding the prestigious Walkley she was awarded for the program

Office work? As easy as scoring a century

All set for yet another backyard Test

'Cheers, Nugget,' from
his irreplaceable mates,
'Mr Jarman', right, and
'Mr Rowe'

The complete cricketer

'Well done, Nug.' Congratulations from the South Australian team after yet another century, this time at the Melbourne Cricket Ground

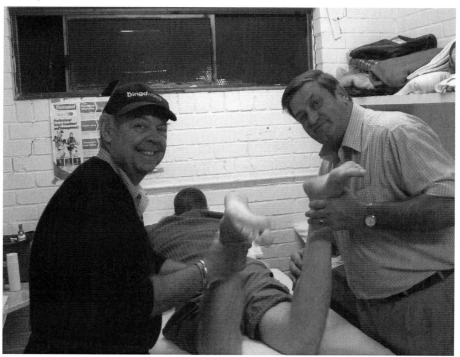

Masseur: assisting good mate Hans Ellenbroek at Goodwood Saints Football Club training

TV 'star': at Channel 7, Adelaide, with Christine Mallett and sports commentator and former squash champion, Chris Dittmar

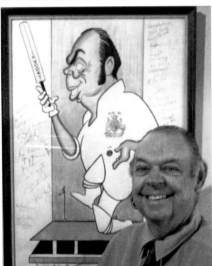

Nugget's character, and also his place in the Australian cricket community, are captured perfectly by Ross Bateup, left, and Michael Atchison

A week after the Crusaders left Windsor Castle, the Queen spoke with the Australian High Commissioner Doug McLelland: 'Doug, I met this incredible Australian character last week. His name is Swan Richards.'

Before the Queen could continue, Doug said, 'We all know Swan Richards. He's a great mate of Ben Humphreys [Veteran Affairs Minister in the Hawke Government]. He used to walk around Parliament House doing what he liked.'

'Did he now?' the Queen mused.

'Yeah, we didn't worry. We all knew Swan. He was also a good mate of Bob Hawke's, they'd get together to pick the Prime Minister's Eleven.'

'He's [Swan] the most incredible fellow with the English language.'

'Yes, your majesty. That's Swan.'

The Queen summoned her Royal Page, John Taylor, and asked, 'Can you tell me next time the Crusaders are coming to Windsor and I'll come down to see them.'[17]

Swan has taken the Crusaders to England on twelve occasions, while the Queen has watched their match against the Royal Household eight times. Former Singapore Airlines boss John MacKinnon, who went on the 1989 tour, recalls when the Queen did not attend: 'Cilla Black turned up in Her Majesty's absence on one occasion, and on the other Richie and Daphne Benaud were present. It was, I think, the time of the Benauds when Swan did his dash. He said some rather uncomplimentary things about the Queen in earshot of members of the Royal Household and Swan and the Crusaders were—sadly—no longer welcome at Windsor Castle.'[18]

Nugget is grateful to Swan for the opportunity to tour England, but he believes Swan should remember those who helped him. Over the past 18 years, Swan hasn't had much to do with Nugget or the old gang at Rowe & Jarman. Nugget isn't angry about Swan's silence. He is sad. 'You would think that after all Mr Rowe and Mr Jarman have done for him, you'd think he'd get in touch sometimes.'

Conversely, the Royal Household continues to keep in touch with Nugget. 'The Royal Household sends me a Christmas card every year.'

It was 10 p.m. on Sunday, July 30, 1989, when Nugget and his fellow Crusaders boarded the Singapore Airlines jet, Flight SQ21, signalling the end of the first Crusaders tour to England.

The Crusaders spent three days in Singapore and much of the time they congregated at the famous Singapore Cricket Club. Nugget was photographed inspecting the pitch before the Crusaders took on the Singapore Cricket Club XI in a one-day match. Nugget stood in the middle of the ground, the same plot of grass which bowed to the might of the invading Japanese army in 1942. Built at the height of

British Imperialism, the Singapore Cricket Club, with its oak-panelled billiard rooms, splendid bars and wicker chairs, became the Japanese army's Officers' Club.

However, in 1989 Singapore was a different world from the horror of the Second World War. Nugget found the club a haven of joy and hospitality. He sipped Tiger beer and watched the Crusaders play brilliant cricket. Then, at the end of their three-day stay, Nugget himself scored a century in oppressive heat before the Crusaders flew home.

On August 3, 1989, Nugget arrived at Adelaide Airport to be greeted by his sister Diane, his brothers-in-law Rusty and Neil, and his long-time friend David 'Tidd' Rowe. Excited to be home, Nugget walked into the arrivals lounge and when he saw his loved ones, his face lit up and he gave them the thumbs up.

He couldn't wait to tell everyone about England, meeting the Queen, seeing Buckingham Palace and Windsor Castle, and, best of all, Lord's Cricket Ground and being with all the Test players, his heroes. But, as always, Nugget was more interested in others and was full of questions.

'How's Mr Jarman? And Russell and Slugger? Everyone at the shop? Are the Magpies still winning?'

He was the same Nugget. England hadn't changed him, just broadened his experience.

Notes

1 Pam Freeman to author, March 2008
2 ibid.
3 ibid.
4 ibid.
5 *Adelaide Advertiser*, March 1, 1965
6 Ashley Mallett, 'Nugget's the name… Cricket's the game', *Hills Gazette,* February 6, 1974
7 Nugget Rees Collection
8 Swan Richards to author, Melbourne, February 2008
9 ibid.
10 Pam Freeman to author, April 2008
11 John MacKinnon to author, March 2008
12 Swan Richards introduction in Crusaders magazine, September 1989
13 Swan Richards to author, Melbourne, February 2008
14 ibid.
15 ibid.
16 Joan Richards to author, October 2007
17 Swan Richards to author, February 2008
18 John MacKinnon to author, April 2008

CHAPTER 5

Nugget and cricket

Barry 'Nugget' Rees has witnessed all the great cricket moments on Adelaide Oval since 1962.

In 1963 Nugget was in the South Australian dressing-room when Garry Sobers asked Les Favell, the SA captain, for permission to wear his West Indies Test cap against the touring South Africans.

'Sure you can, Sobey,' Favell replied. 'I don't care if you wear a fireman's helmet. But why are you wearing your West Indies cap?'

Sobers looked at his State skipper and said with a wry smile, 'I think it is long overdue for these South Africans to have a good, long look at the West Indies logo.'

It was Sobers' personal way of putting it up Apartheid. Nugget nodded knowingly.

Nugget was also present at the Adelaide Oval for every one of Adam 'Gilly' Gilchrist's slamming innings; Mark 'Junior' Waugh's debut Test hundred; and when Doc Beard rushed on to the field to tend to Clive Lloyd, who had dived for a catch and wound up with a badly bruised spleen. He saw David Hookes score a century in 41 deliveries against Victoria; and Nugget was there when Shane Warne bowled Australia to a remarkable victory over England in 2006.

In the summer of 1993–94 he was at the game and with the players in the Australian dressing-room when a courageous last wicket stand between Tim 'Maysie' May and Craig 'Billy the Kid' McDermott came unstuck, with the West Indies winning the Test by one run. With a run to tie and two runs to win, McDermott was given out, caught down leg-side off the bowling of Windies paceman Courtney Walsh. Nugget was sitting beside Test skipper Allan 'AB' Border, who eased his nerves by throwing a ball from hand to hand. Then the last wicket fell with Australia one run short. The TV cameras turned on the players' viewing area and millions of viewers saw Border angrily throw the ball to the floor. When quizzed on what AB said, Nugget replies, 'What happens in the dressing-room remaining in the dressing-room.' Steadfastly remaining loyal to his heroes and mates, Nugget never breaks confidentiality. (Even though thousands of television viewers probably had an inkling of the words AB uttered the instant McDermott fell.)

During Nugget's lengthy association with Adelaide Oval,

he has also seen six Sheffield Shield trophy victories for South Australia.

The first was in 1963–64, soon after Barry Jarman had first taken him down to mix with the State players. On February 25, 1964, just three days before Nugget's 20th birthday, Adelaide's morning broadsheet bore the headline: CHAMPIONS. Les Favell's South Australia team had won the Shield, thanks to a brilliant all-round effort from Garry Sobers who scored 973 runs and took 47 wickets, and Rex 'Sahib' Sellers, a flighty leg-spinner who took 46 wickets, enough to earn him a trip to England with the 1964 Test touring team.

Then, after an absence of five years, in 1968–69, South Australia, still under the leadership of Favell, again won the Shield. Nugget was there to see the last match of the season, in which SA had to beat NSW to claim the trophy. SA dismissed NSW for a paltry 110 in reply to SA's first innings score of 307 (Greg Chappell hit 107). Almost immediately the NSW second innings began, fast-bowler Alan Frost felled NSW batsman John Wilson with a flyer. The ball struck Wilson on the head and he collapsed in a pool of blood, knocking down his stumps as he fell.

The umpire had raised his finger to give Wilson out 'hit-wicket', but the players were all gathered around the injured batsman. Wilson was carried off on a stretcher and Favell, even though his team needed to win outright to secure the Sheffield Shield, went to the umpires and asked them to rescind their decision to give Wilson out.

'If John is fit enough to come back and bat, that's fine by us,' Favell said.

Wilson did return, his head swathed in bandages, and he scored 114, the only first-class century of his career. SA won the game by eight wickets and we all learnt of Favell's sportsmanship that day, but Nugget already knew what calibre of man Les Favell was.

Ian Chappell took over the SA captaincy from Favell, and in 1970–71, under Chappell, SA again won the Shield. South African Barry Richards scored 1145 runs at an average of 104.09. Nugget saw some of Richards' amazing innings and he laughed with us all in the players' viewing area the day Richards, his right thumb badly broken, hit three successive cover-driven boundaries using his left-hand off the bowling of NSW spinner Kerry O'Keeffe.

The next summer, 1971–72, SA lost the Shield trophy by 1 point to WA, before falling on hard times and finishing last in 1974–75. Around this time Nugget began coaching the State cricketers in basketball. We bonded as a team and under Chappell again we turned things around in 1975–76, winning the Shield.

Under the captaincy of David Hookes, SA won the Sheffield Shield in 1981–82. But their next victory was not until 1995–96, this time under the captaincy of Jamie Siddons, the former Victorian right-hand batsman and brilliant fieldsman.

The 95–96 Sheffield Shield final was held at Adelaide Oval against WA; SA only needed to draw the match while WA needed an outright win. With 10 overs to go WA needed just one wicket to win the match and wrest the Shield. Nugget's good mate Peter McIntyre, from the 1989 Crusaders tour, found himself joined by medium-paced bowler Shane George. McIntyre and George had to survive 60 balls—they were the hopes of the side.

Nugget tells the story: 'It was a great win because Peter McIntyre and Shane George had to bat for a fair while. They did. They hung on. WA thought they had the Shield when they appealed for a catch off McIntyre. They thought Macca edged it but he didn't, and the umpire said "Not out". The umpire was right. That was our last Sheffield Shield trophy. We're due for another one soon.'

On February 28, 1994, Nugget turned 50. To celebrate the occasion, a function was held at the Players' Bar in Adelaide. Not surprisingly, the guest list read like a 'Who's Who' of South Australian and Australian sport.

Even Sir Donald Bradman was invited. The Don, however, was unable to attend, as he explained in a letter to Diane, Nugget's sister:

12-1-94

Dear Mrs. Smith,

I thank you for your letter inviting me to attend Nugget's 50th birthday on February 27th but regret that other family commitments will make this impossible. I'll be with him in spirit.

I am glad to know that I have played a small part in Barry's interest in and association with cricket and just hope he will be able to enjoy his participation therein in the years ahead.

Yours sincerely,

(Signed)

Don Bradman

Hundreds turned up at the Players' Bar to pay tribute to their great friend. Nugget took the microphone and he spoke to the audience with passion, revealing an uncanny sense of timing. He had them rolling in the aisles with his one-liners.

Nearly ten years later, another celebration was held in honour of Nugget. And again, the cream of South Australian and Australian sport were there to support the man whom many considered to be an inspiration.

AFL footballer Tony McGuinness first met Nugget in 1985 when he was employed at Rowe & Jarman. In 1986 he left Adelaide to play football with the Western Bulldogs in Melbourne for five years. Upon his return in 1991, McGuinness became a partner in Rowe & Jarman. And he got to know Nugget really well.

McGuinness says: 'In Adelaide the Adelaide Crows were as high profile as the Australian cricket team. When I was captain of the Crows, I'd get used to people saying hello, whether you were walking down the street, or going to the post office. But when I went anywhere with Nugget, dozens of people would stop to speak with him. It was always

Nugget. He was just so incredibly high profile. It would be nothing for fifty, seventy or a hundred people to acknowlede him when you'd go out for an hour.'[1]

McGuinness helped establish the Barry Rees Trust Fund. The fund was set up in the wake of Nugget finishing work with Rowe & Jarman. McGuinness thought such a fund would ease the financial burden on Nugget's family and help pay for a variety of costs associated with Nugget's lifestyle.

To fast-track money for the fund, it was decided to put on a 'Nugget roast'.

McGuinness took Nugget for a coffee and explained how he would arrange a night of prominent sports stars to help raise money to establish his fund. Which sports stars might attend such a function?' McGuinness asked.

'Oh, well, we'd get Dizzy [SA and Test fast-bowler Jason Gillespie], Uncle Boofa [Darren Lehmann] and Hookesy [David Hookes],' Nugget volunteered. 'Chappelli [Ian Chappell] will come over too.'

McGuinness wasn't convinced that the big names would attend, but Nugget knew he would get support from sports heroes throughout the land.

'We'll get Steve Waugh too,' Nugget said confidently.

'C'mon Nug, we've not going to get the Australian cricket captain. It's too big, mate. We can't get him.'

'Yep, we'll get him Freddy [McGuinness' nickname]. I have his number.'

Nugget produced his little black book. And among myriad names and numbers was one for 'S. Waugh'.

'Okay, Nugget. We've got the number, but I can't just ring him.'

Nugget couldn't understand why McGuinness was being so doubtful. Afterall, Steve Waugh was a good mate.

'Okay, Nug, you ring him,' McGuinness dared. 'You ring the captain of the Australian cricket team. You get him on the phone and I shout a beer.'

Nugget rang Steve Waugh and after a minute or two explaining the reason for his call, Waugh indicated to Nugget that he would be involved. With a broad smile and a thumbs up, Nugget put down the phone.

McGuinness was amazed.

'A Night with Nugget' was held before 550 people at the Adelaide Oval on Friday, June 27, 2003.

It was a night to remember. Nugget sat on a throne on stage and beside him were Ian Chappell, Steve Waugh, David Hookes and Merv Hughes. It was clear then that Nugget's heroes held him in the highest esteem.

Former WA and SA batsman James Brayshaw, who once worked alongside Nugget at Rowe & Jarman and is now president of the North Melbourne Football Club, was Master of Ceremonies. David Rowe and Barry Jarman spoke lovingly about Nugget's early days at the shop. And Nugget's mates—Chappelli, Tugga, Hookesy and Big Merv—'roasted' Nugget in the most generous manner after high-profile personalities were interviewed by Brayshaw. Just as Nugget emits an aura of love, there was a reciprocal atmosphere of love towards the man of the moment, emanating from every person present.

Sports memorabilia was auctioned and a lot of material had been donated. Cricket Australia and the SACA helped in this way and that swelled the coffers of the Barry Rees Trust Fund.

Nugget was presented with a Tribute Book, signed by many people. Here is a selection of their comments:

'Congratulations on your great career, work, rest and play, talk football and cricket. Best team man, B.O.G. Well done—FAT BOY!'—Hans Ellenbroek.

'Nugget, Congratulations big boy! What a champion night for a champion bloke. All the best, much, much from your mate'—Tony ('Fred') McGuinness.

'Dear Barry, Your dinner was one of the highlights of our life. Congratulations, you are the best! How proud your dad and mum would be of you and your wonderful achievements. Well done'—Aunty Paula (Paula Keily).

'Nugget, What a great night for a fantastic bloke in life. Kind regards always'—Steve Renfrey.

'Nugget, Thanks for your friendship over many years. Your positive attitude is an inspiration to us all. Good health and best wishes'—Russell Ebert and the Ebert family.

'To Sir Nugget, You deserve a knighthood for your contribution to cricket and football. Love ya work'—Tim Ginever.

'Nugget, You are the king and always a true friend. Look after yourself and your family. Your true mate'—Boofa (Darren Lehmann).

When Nugget reflects on that amazing night, he thinks of those no longer with us and especially David Hookes. 'That was the last time I saw Hookesy,' he says, his eyes welling.

In the Wendy Page-produced *Australian Story* featuring Nugget, one important point that came through loud and clear was the reciprocal love between Nugget and the Test players. Wendy was astounded by the attitude of these international sportsmen towards Nugget. 'It is warm and loving and very genuine,' she said.[2]

In January 2004, Jason 'Dizzy' Gillespie arranged for Nugget to be flown to Sydney and be a part of the SCG Test against India. It was the final Test of the Australia–India series and Steve Waugh's last Test match.

'It was terrific,' Nugget recalls. 'I stayed in the same room as Dizzy and his wife, Anna, but I was given instructions to not get out of bed before 7 a.m. I woke up early, but I didn't wake them.

'Dizzy gave me his Test shirt at the Adelaide Test and Binga [Brett Lee] gave me a pair of cricket boots. And the shoes I wore were the ones Gilly [Adam Gilchrist] gave me a couple of seasons ago. My batting gloves came from Greg Blewett at the end of a Sheffield Shield match. My bat was from Punter [Ricky Ponting]. And I wore the 1964 baggy-green cap that Mr Jarman gave me a long time ago.'

Nugget also had the honour of taking the drinks out on to the SCG during the time the Australians were in the field.

Nugget reckons Steve Waugh would have scored a hundred in his last Test innings, but for a good catch by Sachin Tendulkar in the outfield. 'I would have liked Stephen to have made a ton. Tendulkar did the wrong thing—he should have dropped the catch.'

Steve Waugh's manager, Robert Joske told the media at the time: 'Nugget's here because he's been such a big part of Stephen's life. He's a very special person in all the cricketers' lives. He's an institution in Adelaide and he's been there since day one of Stephen's career there.'[3]

Nugget attended the skipper's last Test press conference. Long after the press dispersed came a lovely gesture from the retiring Australian Test captain. Nugget recalls: 'Stephen said to me, "It has been great having you here, Nugget." Then he said, "C'mon Nugget, let's go out for a last look." And I walked out to the wicket with Tugga and his wife, Lynette. He has always been a good friend and a good fella. I don't think he's changed.'

In his autobiography, *Out of the Comfort Zone*, Waugh tells of that special moment when Nugget was with him in the centre of the SCG: 'Hours later, with the crowd gone, I walked back out onto the hallowed turf and inspected the pitch for one final time. With me were Lynette and the legendary Barry "Nugget" Rees, a bloke who is special in every way. Jason Gillespie had organized for Nugget to travel from Adelaide to cheer me on in my final Test.

'Now, as I surveyed the worn and dusty foot-holes and cracks that meandered along the entirety of the pitch, I saw Nugget play an imaginary defensive shot with the same dreams I had harboured as a kid.'[4]

After they returned from their last nostalgic look at the SCG pitch, Nugget joined all the Australian players at Steve Waugh's private party.

What a week it had been for Nugget. If only his dad could see him now.

But Nugget says, 'Dad knows... Dad knows...'

For many years, Darren Lehmann, the man Nugget calls 'Uncle Boof', has been Nugget's friend and confidant. One wintry Wednesday morning, Nugget and I had a long chat with Uncle Boof at a Hutt Street cafe in Adelaide.

Darren Lehmann was a young champion. At the tender age of 17 he took the Adelaide cricket scene by storm by hitting a double century for Salisbury in the district competition and he was immediately earmarked for stardom. Lehmann played his first match for SA in 1987 under the captaincy of his hero David Hookes. Nugget, of course, watched that game. He knew all about the young, thickset left-hander who used a cricket bat like a sledge hammer.

Lehmann recalls: 'I first met Nugget when I was playing for Salisbury against Kensington and I thought "Who is this lunatic?" I've known Nugget ever since I got into the State scene and learnt all the background about him from Hookesy and the older players and about BJ's influence. It was one of those chance meetings in life, but knowing Nugget has been a great for my life and for my family.'[5]

Lehmann, who featured in the *Australian Story* about Nugget, says: 'Nugget is as loyal a person as you could possible get. He would do anything for you. I couldn't imagine life without him. Once you retire you don't see him as often, but you see him often enough.

'Nug's a special person in my life and my family's life and he has been so throughout the years. Kids love him, everyone loves him and that's the problem—sometimes he doesn't shut up. It's the greatest thing that he endears himself to so many people.

'Obviously cricket and football are his passions, but you go to Goodwood Saints, or the Colonel Light Gardens RSL Club, they treat him just the same. They all love him. At least he's slowed down his drinking. Nugget was diagnosed with diabetes some ten years ago. He has religiously stuck to a diet ever since. Nowadays Nug will have a diet beer and/or a glass of red wine—and , no more.'[6]

Lehmann senses a slight change of mood among the SA players, and adds some words of caution. 'I've noticed we are losing the tradition of Nugget travelling away with us.

To be fair, the Redbacks have been pretty good and I hope the tradition continues for a while to come.'[7]

So what exactly is Lehmann driving at? 'I think what happens is that everyone moves on and changes direction and sometimes youngsters don't understand the whole concept of life,' he says. 'Nugget Rees going away with the State team is, as John Inverarity would say, "a rite of passage".'[8]

The tradition of Nugget with the team in all Adelaide Oval matches and touring to at least one State match during any given summer has become a constant in an ever-increasing change of way of life in the sport of cricket.

Lehmann says: 'It has always been a case of Nug's here and he is part of the team. And it was made perfectly clear to me—by the older blokes like Barry Jarman and David Hookes—and you understood very quickly that Nugget was a big part of what happens in the SA cricket team environment. You understood it and you embraced it. That was the greatest thing; you embraced the whole concept of Nugget's involvement. I hope that continues for as long as Nugget is alive.'[9]

Lehmann believes Nugget is the most positive person he's known around the cricket team. 'Even when SA was faced with the most impossible situation, Nugget believed that we could win. Whenever I failed, he came up and said, "Don't worry Uncle Boof, you'll get a hundred next time."

'I think the best thing about Nugget is that he puts life

into perspective for you as a cricketer—he brings you down to earth very quickly.

'Cricket was very much a roller-coaster. When I was a youngster and got out, I used to get pretty angry. As you get older, you deal with it a bit better. Nug helps you through that when you're a youngster. He's fantastic with the young blokes. A youngster would get out cheaply and Nugget would be there alongside him, he'd sit with him and console him. And he knows more about the young blokes coming into the team than we do. He knows their record, almost like an Indian, in a way. The Indian supporters know more about you and your record than you know yourself.'[10]

I posed the question. 'You're not an Indian, are you Nug?'

'Oh, no. No, I'm not an Indian!' Nug laughed.

Lehmann then looked over his cup of coffee, setting his eyes squarely on Nugget. 'The scariest thing for me—everyone passes on in this world, simply a fact of life—but when Nug does pass away, and I hope it's not for 20 or 30 years or however long it's going to be, he'll leave a big hole in everyone's life, not just mine or my family's but everyone who has come into contact with him. He'll have a bigger funeral than David Hookes or Sir Donald Bradman, all those blokes...'[11]

Lehmann breaks into a huge grin. 'Hey, Nug, you're not going to die yet?'

'No thanks, not yet,' Nugget grins back.

When Wendy Page was putting together her story on Nugget for the *Australian Story* feature, she pondered over John Inverarity's words, where he spoke in like terms to Lehmann. 'When Nugget finally does pass away, there won't be standing room at Adelaide Oval.'[12]

The meeting with Lehmann was good for me, for here were two cricketers from different eras. Our common ground was obviously the game of cricket, but the man who brought us together was the great facilitator of love and friendship, Barry 'Nugget' Rees.

Nugget and I had arrived at the cafe before Lehmann. When Uncle Boof turned up, I shook hands with him then watched as the pair of them hugged. Lehmann explained: 'We always have a big hug when we meet. Just like what happened here today. You just want to grab him, hold him, cuddle him. And when you have a photograph with him, he always makes you happy. He's never made anyone unhappy.

'He's good to be around. Nug's never got a negative thought, apart from when he goes off about the umpiring, even when they are totally right.

'Nug knew exactly how I felt when I came off the ground, especially when I was captain. He knew my mood better than the other players; he always knew when I was happy, when I was steaming.'[13]

Lehmann's last summer was extraordinary given that he was stripped of the SA captaincy and midway through the season was virtually forced out of the game. 'I wasn't enjoying it,' he reveals. 'I couldn't stand all the rubbish going on at the SACA, so I opted out.'[14]

And out he went—with a bang, scoring a big century in his final Sheffield Shield match and a century in his one-day finale. He didn't have to say a word.

'Hookesy once told me to "Leave them wanting more". And I guess I achieved that,' Lehmann says. 'On the last day I spoke to each player individually, but the hardest thing for me was to say goodbye, from a cricket point of view, to Nug. We both had tears in our eyes.'[15]

But Nugget has remained a vital part of Darren Lehmann's post-cricket life. 'Nugget stays at our place once a year. He gives us a wake-up call about 6 a.m. The greatest thing our kids learn from Nugget is respect—respect for an elder.

'His manners—they are free. Aren't they, Nug? Manners are free?'[16]

Nugget gives a double thumbs up, and says, 'That's right.'

'Send Nug on an errand and it would be done. But you had to specify if the errand was urgent. If you told him that the job was urgent and had to be done straightaway, it was done. However, if you told him to take his time, he did. He'd be talking to everyone to and from where he had to go and would take ages to return.

'Then there's the speeches on the table, his batting and all those runs, the fun having an ice bath, but there are some things we can't print, eh Nug?'

Another thumbs up.

Nugget then asked: 'Uncle Boof, how do you think I'll get on with Younis Khan?' (the Pakistani batsman who was recruited to play for South Australia in 2008–09).

'You'll get on fine, Nug. He's very "westernised". Warney [Shane Warne] told me he was terrific.'[17]

Throughout the chat with Uncle Boof there is light-hearted banter, but there's also an underlying seriousness about what Nugget brings to those around him. Lehmann says: 'Nug allows you to show emotion. He actually encourages you to show emotion.

'Back in the old days, a man showing emotion was a bit of a no-no, but it still happened, though very rarely. Now it happens more and more. Nugget breaks down the macho barrier better than you or I could do it, and he encourages you to show emotion and to be unafraid to be emotional.

'That's not an easy thing for a man in this day and age, but with Nug it just happens.'[18]

Nugget's legend is such that some have been inspired to write of the man in verse.

Dave Parkinson is one such example. Parkinson opened the batting for Kensington, Nugget's beloved 'Browns', and ran a sporting goods agency. Affectionately and widely known as 'DH', Parkinson penned these lines in tribute to Nugget.

Nugget

Barry Rees, affectionately known as Nugget
A remarkable sporting character.
Mild mannered with loyalty unsurpassed,
His love of cricket hard to deter.
Australian cricketers enjoy his presence,
His enthusiasm and loyalty unique.
With encouragement to players heartfelt
His goal an Aussie victory to seek.
The Redbacks are his domestic commitment
Kensington his grade club well supported.
His attendance at games regular and sincere
Each player acknowledged and roundly exhorted.
Suitably attired for each occasion,
Proudly sporting the team's official garb.
Cheering with gusto he urges the side,
Neatly deflecting the occasional barb.
His cricket gear is packed in reserve
Ready when the Test is completed.
Padded up he strides to the wicket
His century is achieved and undefeated.
Nugget is the embodiment of simplicity.
A naïve man with a precious gift.
The gift of an unassuming lifestyle
His fellowship gives everyone a lift.
(© David 'DH' Parkinson)

In 1996, former NSW batsman Neil 'Harpo' Marks (the brother of Lynn 'Full' Marks, who played for NSW and SA in the 1960s) rang Barry Jarman heralding his intention to write a chapter on Nugget in his proposed book. Neil's book, *Tales for All Seasons*, hit the book stores in 1997, the same year the Port Adelaide Football Club became part of the Australian Football League as Port Power and Nugget immediately dropped off the Crows. His heart was always with Port—the Magpies—and it is now with the Power.

Neil Marks' own story is remarkable. Neil played just ten matches for NSW, hitting 568 runs at an average of 47.33, including 180 not out in his Sheffield Shield debut and 103 in the next match, before his first-class cricket career was cut short by an operation for a hole in the heart. He then developed into a skilled wordsmith, wielding a pen as deftly as he cover-drove a cricket ball.

Nugget is featured in the Marks' book alongside such household names as Bradman and Phar Lap. Marks wrote of Nugget in a loving and respectful tone, and ended his chapter on our 'Man for all seasons' with the following tribute.

Ode to Nugget

In Adelaide, a legend, by the name of Nugget Rees
Sits and watches flannelled players on the green
He is loyal, he is loved and he always tries to please,
He's a man who is endemic to the scene.

Though he's never been selected, nor made a first-class ton
And he doesn't work out tactics for the side,
He is the man behind the SACA who cheers their every run
And imbues them with an energy and pride.
When sitting in the viewing room, he's given pride of place
And he wears his SACA shirt just like the best,
Although he's not athletic he displays a certain grace,
Still retaining youth's vitality and zest.
He's seen the Chappell brothers and he's watched
    the brothers Waugh,
He saw Sobers play with strength and charm and ease.
He's watched so many legends—but there's always room for more,
For he loves the game of cricket, Nugget Rees.
But when the summer's over and the chill sou-easter blows,
'Take the mark, Chris' all the crowd hear Nugget cry,
Though his heart is with the Magpies, he barracks for the Crows
And his spirit soars whenever the big men fly.
He cheers for Chris McDermott, Tony Modra and the rest,
Nugget's always there in winter's wind and rain.
An inclination tells him it's the game he loves the best
And I guess he does—till summer comes again.
But Nugget is a sportsman who's oblivious to code,
For no matter where he goes he finds a friend.
Though maybe through life's journey Nugget walks
    a diff'rent road,
He will turn up at 'a good place' in the end.
He's met Australia's heroes and the man out on The Mound

Nugget and cricket

And he knows the bloke who tries to take him down,

But in his wide experience old Nugget's always found

That a smile will serve him better than a frown.

He loves his mates, the players, and the fans he walks among,

To Nugget every day is fresh and new.

He is waved to by the members, chased after by the young

So he stops to sign an autograph or two.

Everybody calls him Nugget, he's loved by one and all.

For he always does the very best he can.

He'll be part of sport's tradition, while there's a bat and a ball,

He's a sportsman, he's a legend—he's a man.

(©Neil 'Harpo' Marks)[19]

I decided to complete this hat-trick of Nugget verse with my own, home-spun delivery:

Nugget, the champ

A heart of gold; a batsman bold

For Nugget Rees this story's told.

Our lives enriched by Nugget's style

That beaming face, that loving smile.

Dizzy and Rowdy and Pommies forlorn

There's BJ, and TJ, and Tugga Waugh

Hans and Super and much, much more.

There's Nugget beside us clapping each run

Boof catches his eye; thumbs up in a blink

Nug's eye on the play, the game in the pink.

———

Nugget Rees

For forty-odd years Nug's been on the case
Nugget's a star of the human race.
(© Ashley Mallett 2008)

Sprightly and articulate, 94-year-old retired school teacher Phyllis Golding lives directly across the road from Nugget's family home in Colonel Light Gardens. Every Monday evening, without fail, Nugget goes over to Phyllis' house and takes out her rubbish bins, and every Tuesday morning, again without fail, he brings them back in for her.

Phyllis explains, with a smile: 'Barry used to look after Joan, a lady down the road. He'd go there and have coffee with her and look after the rubbish bins, but she contracted cancer and died. Since Joan died, Barry has been coming over here, taking the rubbish bins in and out for me and having morning coffee.'[20]

Tuesdays with Nugget has become a regular and delightful event for Phyllis. Nugget, of course, loves the involvement. He is in his element when he gets the chance to help people.

Nugget returns the rubbish bins to their rightful spots, then he knocks at the back door.

Nugget always knocks, he never presumes.

'Oh it's you, Nugget. Come in dear.'

'I've brought someone with me to meet you,' Nugget says enthusiastically.

We sit at the kitchen table. Phyllis tells Nugget to make the coffee.

'Barry always makes the coffee,' she says. 'He does a good job and is very good at making people comfortable.'

Nug boils the kettle. 'Can I get you something, my dear? Tea? Coffee?' he asks Phyllis.

Phyllis tells him that a jar of his 'special' biscuits are in the cupboard. Nugget smiles and pats Phyllis on the shoulder.

'Thank you, my dear, thank you... much, much.'

The kettle boils, Nugget makes Phyllis her cup of tea and makes me coffee, and with his 'special' sugar-free biscuits in their blue tin placed on the table, we're set for a chat.

Nugget tells Phyllis of the impending book on his life and her face beams.

'It's all about cricket and football,' Nugget says.

'Oh, that's wonderful,' Phyllis replies excitedly. 'It will be a terrific story.'

Nugget looks across the kitchen table and says, 'Rowdy, can we play a match? Two of the great teams playing in a match?'

A match? I'm not sure about the wisdom of playing a match because some of the players Nugget is sure to throw my way when we pick the sides are probably beyond playing competitive cricket.

As sole selector Nugget finds it difficult to trim the number of players in each team.

'Some batsmen, Nug?'

'Ah, Justin Langer, and Adam Gilchrist—he could play as a batsman, is that okay?'

'Fine Nug, but what do we do with Rodney Marsh, Barry Jarman, Brian Taber, Ian Healy, Graham Manou, Brad Haddin and Wally Grout? We need two well-balanced elevens.'

He discounts the fact that some of the people he chooses have passed away. 'Well, I'd like Les Favell to lead my side, then Darren Lehmann, Langer, Gilchrist, Neil Harvey, Doug Walters, David Hookes, Greg Ritchie, Richie Benaud, Ashley Mallett, Wally Grout, Ian Healy, Craig McDermott, Merv Hughes, Paul Sheahan, Neil Hawke, Eric Freeman, Max Walker and Stuart MacGill.'

Nugget has named nineteen players, excluding himself. Then he adds Ian Davis, Rick McCosker and Don Bradman.

'Rowdy, can we have Bradman? I mean, it was a long time go.'

Yes, Don Bradman is fine. Then I tell him, 'You'll be opening with Les Favell, followed by Don Bradman, then Darren Lehmann.'

His face lights up and I get the thumbs up. Nug likes the start of the batting order.

'I'm glad to see Stuart MacGill in the team,' Nug volunteers from left-field. 'You might know that he is hard to handle, but I handle him well.'

'Just how do you handle Magilla?' I ask.

'I am the only one about the team who can handle him,' Nugget explains. 'I sit him down and talk to him quietly. It calms him.'

Phyllis and I don't doubt it; if anyone can calm Stuart MacGill it is Barry 'Nugget' Rees.

There are 25 names in our opposing team: Ian Redpath, Matthew Hayden, Ian Chappell, Greg Chappell, Mark Waugh, Steve Waugh, Tom Vievers, Gary Cosier, Ross Edwards, Alan Davidson, Norm O'Neill, Ken Cunningham, Jim Burke, John Inverarity, Terry Jenner, Jason Gillespie, Dennis Lillee, Jeff Thomson, Rod Marsh, David Boon, Tim May, Brian Booth, Peter Burge, Bill Lawry and Brett Lee.

Who are the players to be axed?

'I can't drop anyone,' Nugget says, adding that 'Mr Jarman has to play. I find it hard to leave anyone out. Would they be upset?'

To Nugget, all the players he has known over the years are his mates. And he remains totally loyal to them.

We went on for most of the morning trying to trim the squads, but to no avail. For Nugget to get his match we would need the rules of cricket to be changed, and we didn't have time to put a proposal to Lord's.

I pointed out to Nugget that there was a game in the 19th century when the All England Eleven played Twenty-Two of Kent and Twenty-Two of Scotland. And in 1861 H.H. Stephenson's England Eleven played Twenty-Two of NSW and Twenty-Two of Victoria. 'There might be a chance that the MCC would allow two teams of 22 players,' I suggested. But Nugget could not contemplate dropping any men whatsoever, so the whole idea was lost.

Besides, Nugget wasn't finished. 'We can't forget Glenn McGrath and Warney. They've got to play—in my side.'

While Nugget revels in the modern era, he didn't forget some of the players from the recent and distant past. 'What about Ray Lindwall and Keith Miller, Bill Johnston, Rodney Hogg? Shaun Tait? Andrew Hilditch?'

'What about TJ?' I asked.

'Oh, he's on the other side.'

'And Warney?'

'He's got to be on my side. Steve Waugh on my side and Mark Waugh on the other side.'

Nugget also picked a barrage of pace bowlers on the other side—Lillee, Davidson, Thomson and Gillespie—for a very good reason.

'It will be a challenge,' he laughed. 'I'll be opening with Les Favell and when the spinner comes on he'll be singing "Happy Birthday".'

Nugget then related the tale of Favell batting in Perth against a young spinner. The WA captain Barry Shepherd threw Terry Jenner the ball and Favell, at the striker's end, started singing 'Happy Birthday to you, Les Favell, Happy birthday to you'.

As Jenner was about to deliver that first ball, Favell charged down the track, singing 'Happy Birthday' all the way and met the ball on the full, smashing it over cover, one bounce for four.

Shepherd moved John Parker back at cover to a position right on the fence.

Favell started singing louder. John Inverarity at first slip was laughing so much there were tears in his eyes, making it difficult to see anything. Jenner came in again and Favell charged down the wicket, again he hit the ball on the full and it careered over cover one bounce to the man on the fence.

Ian Chappell, who was at the other end, ran through, but Favell didn't move from his crease. In fact his back was turned as he ensured his bat was behind the popping crease. Without turning his back, he yelled, 'Piss off Chappelli! It's my birthday, not yours!'

By the time Nugget finished his selections, we had enough players to form at least four first-class elevens. The match was called off, but it was great to hear Nugget talking about his heroes.

When there is no State match at Adelaide Oval, you'll find Nugget watching the Browns (Kensington Cricket Club). There he has seen a cavalcade of cricketers, including Mr Jarman, Greg Blewett, Dean Waugh, Peter Sleep, Terry Jenner, David Parkinson, Peter Brinsley and Sam Parkinson. Nugget remembers most 'home' matches being played at Parkinson Oval. In the days of Bradman and Grimmett,

Kensington Oval was the Browns' home base, but in the 1960s it became a ground for track and field. Recently, however, it has been restored to being a cricket ground.

When Nugget watches the Browns play, he wears the Kensington cap and when the Redbacks play Nug dons the SA cap, but when Australia takes on whoever at the Adelaide Oval for the annual Test match, Nugget wears his 1964 'N.C. O'Neill' baggy-green.

Nugget's baggy-green was given to him by Barry Jarman in 1964. Inside the cap was the name 'N.C. O'Neill' and Nugget took some persuading by Jarman to convince him that the cap was indeed the one he swapped with O'Neill on the 1964 tour of England.

Norm O'Neill was a handsome, big driving, right-hand batsman, who early in his career was labelled the 'new Bradman'. Jarman and O'Neill became life-long friends and annually Norm and his wife Gwen would spend a few days with Barry and Gaynor Jarman on Jar's houseboat, *Gooda's Gold*. Frequently, Lindsay 'Spinner' Kline, the left-arm wrist spinner with the kangaroo hop who took a Test hat-trick against South Africa in 1957–58, and former Test fast-bowler Ian Meckiff, the man SA-based umpire Colin Egar no-balled for throwing in a Test against South Africa in Brisbane in December 1963, joined the Jarmans and the O'Neill's on *Gooda's Gold*.

Sadly, O'Neill contracted throat cancer and after being ill for many years he died at the age of 71.

A couple of years before O'Neill passed away, he and his wife were relaxing over a drink on the deck of *Gooda's Gold* with the Klines and the Jarmans. The subject got around to the increasing popularity of the baggy-green.

Jarman recalls Norm saying that 'years ago a NSW player told me that there was a bloke running about Adelaide Oval wearing my 1964 Test cap'. Norm then lamented that he had no Test cap in his possession.

Jarman, of course, knew that Nugget had the baggy-green with 'N.C. O'Neill' inside and so he went to Nugget and asked if he could have it, faithfully promising Nugget that he would replace the cap with another baggy-green, one with 'B.N. Jarman' inside.

Back on the houseboat in 2006, Jarman presented the 1964 N.C. O'Neill baggy-green to it's original owner, much to Norm's surprise and utter delight. And true to his word, Jarman gave Nugget another baggy-green and even arranged for the year—1964—to be sewn in gold thread on the front, just under the Australian Coat of Arms.

Both Norm O'Neill and Nugget Rees were happy with the outcome.

Nugget's performance at the crease are legendary amongst the Australian cricketers.

As Dennis Lillee says, 'Nugget's scored more runs than Bradman. He has belted all the bowlers about the place. He's even scored hundreds against Glenn McGrath and Shane Warne.'[21]

Who could forget Nugget's magnificent 217 at the MCG in 1970–71? Nugget's feet moved in the sparkling manner of Don Bradman at his peak and his double century came with a resounding cover drive for four, one of many in that eight-minute knock. As he walked from the field, the MCG members rose and applauded. Nugget raised his bat, as he always did when scoring an epic hundred, but this occasion was especially memorable, being his first double century.

But a few weeks later, Nugget, like all great batsmen, hit a rough patch in form. He was batting against Terry 'TJ' Jenner in the nets in Perth.

Nugget was batting well though his timing was uncharacteristically astray. He always picked the wrong 'un, dispatching it ruthlessly through leg for a boundary. TJ's leg-break, too, was a piece of cake. But it was the leg-break which didn't turn, especially the one pitched a shade outside off-stump, which Nugget had to be careful about. I warned Nug not to try and cut the ball that was too close to off-stump.

Nugget reached 99 in quick time. An appeal for a stumping when he was 54 fell on the deaf ears of 'Umpire' Ken Cunningham, but with one run to his hundred, Nugget was out. He tried to cut against a non-turning leg-break, got a bottom edge and chopped the ball on to his stumps.

Nugget looked to square leg where he thought Umpire Cunningham might show compassion for his misfortune and call a no-ball. But the umpire stood impassively, then shrugged his shoulders.

'I'm sorry Mr Batsman but you are out, bowled. Please do not delay heading for the pavilion.'

Nugget never argued. As he walked away he took off his SA cap, shook his head and, eyes welling, he fought back the tears.

Throughout his batting career Nugget has experience many close calls. On one occasion, when Doug Walters was leading NSW, the game was over early, so it was decided that Nugget would bat. The NSW players lined up and clapped Nugget onto the SCG and the umpires walked out to the centre to re-set the stumps.

Nugget hit a century, but not before Walters just missed the SA batsman's head with a searing bouncer.

'Wosh, wosh, woshker!' Nugget-speak for 'a close call'.

Years later, in 1989, Nugget survived a close call of another kind.

The NSW–SA Sheffield Shield game had been interrupted by rain. While the grounds staff were taking off the covers and preparing the wet outfield for a possible start later that morning, the SA players took the opportunity to give Nugget a hit. When the SA players and Nugget ventured onto the field, the NSW boys, most of whom knew Nugget and loved him, followed suit. Again Nugget proved a mighty batsman and within minutes he had smashed another century. The electronic scoreboard flashed on the big screen '100

CONGRATULATIONS NUGGET' and the batsman proudly raised his bat and did so to every section of the crowd.

But as Nugget walked through the gate, held open by Mark 'Junior' Waugh, Waugh had a word with him.

Nugget recalls, 'Junior asked me if I had a medical certificate—wosh wosh woshka.'

Waugh explained that the current ACB ruling over cricketing footwear banned the use of rubber-soled shoes unless the player possessed a medicate certificate.

'Nugget, you are not wearing springs,' Waugh said with a straight face. 'Therefore, I am afraid, your century will not count.'

The case was brought before the match referee, former NSW and Test umpire Ted Wykes. There was considerable argument, although Nugget was unusually subdued. He feared that this just might be the 'century that got away'.

Wykes informed both defendant and plaintiff that 'This is a difficult case and I require 24 hours to consider my decision.'

Nugget spent a sleepless night at the SA team hotel.

Next morning, at precisely 9.30 a.m., 'Judge' Wykes gave a lengthy deliberation to the packed court. Players from both sides sat on the edge of their seats. Nugget was silent.

'Will the defendant please rise?'

Nugget stood, head slightly bowed, hands by his side.

Judge Wykes began: 'Nugget, I find that you did the right thing in wearing rubber springs. The ground was still wet and by wearing rubber-soled shoes you will have done the least damage to the turf. Your century stands.'

The court room erupted in laughter and there were handshakes all round. Nugget had another ton to add to his growing list.

Nugget recalls the Adelaide Oval curator, Les Burdett, lobbying to have rubber-soled cricket boots banned from first-class matches because they caused the grass to 'burn off', unlike steel spikes which broke up and 'aerated' the surface of the pitch.

In the summer of 1995–96, the season SA last won the Sheffield Shield, the Sri Lankan off-spinner Muttiah Murilitharan was no-balled for throwing on seven separate occasions, including by Umpire Darryl Hair in the Boxing Day Test match of 1995.

In his autobiography, Shane Warne defended Hair's right to call a bowler: 'I felt sorry for the bowler [Murilitharan]. To have your action questioned in front of so many people like that amounts to public humiliation. There are ways and means of doing something and I am not sure this was the best solution to a difficult problem. But Hair was right. If an umpire thinks a bowler has a suspect action then it is his duty to call him... Now that the ICC has officially cleared Murilitharan's action we all know where we stand.'[22]

A year after Hair called Murilitharan in Melbourne, he found himself in the Sri Lankan's shoes.

Queensland had been playing South Australia in Brisbane

and Hair was officiating in the game. Queensland won the match convincingly to notch a berth in the Sheffield Shield final, but it was Umpire Hair who ensured the Gabba crowd got their money's worth on the last day of the match.

Immediately swing bowler Adam Dale dismissed the SA number eleven, Paul Wilson, to skittle the visitors for 198, SA captain Jamie Siddons called for Nugget Rees to bat. Trevor Barsby, who was playing his final first-class match at home (he finished his career in the Shield final against WA in Perth a week later), switched roles with Hair. Barsby umpired and Hair bowled.

Nugget belted every one of Hair's deliveries to the Gabba fence, but the highlight of the game, both for Nugget and for the appreciative crowd, was when Hair was no-balled for throwing.

After the game, the Gabba scoreboard flashed 'Tanks for the Memories' as the veteran Queensland opener Barsby walked from the field. Then, within a few minutes the board said 'Well done Nugget—another 100'.

Darren Lehmann recalls that game: 'We [SA] were eight down for not many the night before, so the last morning the game was pretty much all over. I spoke to Stewart Law, the Queensland captain, and he agreed that Nugget could come out to join whoever was the not-out batsman.

'Nug batted beautifully with Brad Young and the Queenslanders throwing everything at them, but couldn't get either of the batsmen out. There was Carl Rackemann along with many of the big name players, bowling their hearts out in their efforts to get Nug out. He played them all with ease. Brad Young stayed long enough for Nug to get his hundred and then the pair called it a day. It was time for lunch.'[23]

When you probe Nugget about Murali's action he laughs and gives you a shadow bent-elbow delivery. 'Mr Jarman thinks he [Murali] throws. I do too,' Nug says steadfastly.

Nugget's perception and knowledge of the game of cricket is astounding.

Some time back former Australia Test team coach John Buchanan interviewed Nugget for inclusion in a book titled *Learning from Legends*. Buchanan asked Nugget a variety of questions, including his take on who might take over from Ricky Ponting as the next Australian captain.

Nugget said: 'Pup [Michael Clarke] will get the job. I think he's shown a lot of promise. A lot of good players like Darren Lehmann and Ricky Ponting have come out and said that Pup's a very, very good player and I think he's got the material to be a very good skipper... but not for a while yet.'[24]

Asked about the captaincy attributes of Mark Taylor as compared with Steve Waugh, Ricky Ponting and Adam Gilchrist, Nugget said: 'Mark was stronger. He was an aggressive captain and he always thought of the players and I thought he did a very good job. The players respected him and he was a very good player. When he came out to bat, he always, you know, made his opponents earn his wicket. He would never give it away easily.'[25]

Nugget knows all his favourite cricketers, past and present, by their nicknames: Favelli, Sobey, Gilly, Parky, BJ, TJ, Sheffield, Fritz, Hawkeye, Hookesy, Boof, Flipper, Dizzy, Rowdy, Digger, Scatters, Gregor, Groover, Invers, Evil, Splinter, Fang, KG, Chappelli, Glue, Bunter, Freddie, Freddy, Sahib, Nodda, FOT, Two-Up, Super, Punter, Warney, JL, Haydos, Pup, Tugga, Magilla, Lennie, Fox, Crayfish, Sos, Chops, Tabsy, Sticks, Spud, Cracker, Slasher, Normie, the Favourite, Glad Bags, Deano, Simmo, Bacchus, Beatle, Garth, Phantom, Al Pal, the Mule, Davo, Stumper, CHO, Timbers, Wizard, Mr Cricketer, Mocca, Mary, Skull, Jimmy, Clakka, Fat Cat, Junior, Cacca, AB, Effie, Stumpy, Full, Harpo, Rocket, Fitteren, Roo, Brute, Tank, Ogo and, of course his namesake, Nugget.

(Their real names in order: Les Favell, Sir Garfield Sobers, Adam Gilchrist, Sam Parkinson, Barry Jarman, Terry Jenner, Alan Shiell, Eric Freeman, Neil Hawke, David Hookes, Darren Lehmann, Wayne Phillips, Jason Gillespie, Ashley Mallett, Andrew Hilditch, Geoff Attenborough, Greg Chappell, Clive Lloyd, John Inverarity, David Sincock, Ashley Woodcock, Wayne Prior, Ken Cunningham, Ian Chappell, Barry Richards, Eddie Barlow, Doug Walters, Andrew Flintoff, Rex Sellers, Neil Dansie, Dennis Lillee, Jeff Thomson, Martin Kent, Ricky Ponting, Shane Warne, Justin Langer, Matthew Hayden,

Michael Clarke, Steve Waugh, Stuart MacGill, Len Pascoe, David Colley, Jeff Hammond, Mick Malone, Howard Mutton, Brian Taber, Ian Brayshaw, Keith Slater, Trevor Hohns, Ken Mackay, Norman O'Neill, Johnny Martin, Jimmy Higgs, Dean Jones, Bobby Simpson, Rod Marsh, Graeme Watson, Graham McKenzie, Bill Lawry, Alan Connolly, Bruce Francis, Alan Davidson, Steve Rixon, Johnny Gleeson, Paul Sheahan, Ian Davis, Mike Hussey, Carl Rackemann, Geoff Dymock, Kerry O'Keeffe, Mike Hendricks, Graham Clarke, Greg Ritchie, Mark Waugh, Rick Darling, Allan Border, Barry Curtin, Bruce Laird, Lynn Marks, Neil Marks, Tony Mann, Alan Turner, Bruce Yardley, Steve Bernard, Trevor Barsby, John MacLean and Keith Miller.)

There are more, but as I kept telling him, we're not compiling a telephone book.

For many of these players, Nugget has been an integral part of their careers. He has been there at the beginning, when they made their first-class debuts, and he has been there when they played their last games.

Port Adelaide and South Australian right-hand batsman, Barry Curtin, played 18 State matches for SA. His introduction to the Sheffield Shield team was at the height of Ian Chappell's reign as State captain. Curtin says: 'I'll never forget the first day of my first game. Just before we are due to walk out onto the field, Ian Chappell puts this bloke called Nugget onto the dressing-room table. That blew me away. I thought, "Am I at the right ground?"

'Nugget gave us all a good talking to—keep your throws up to the keeper, watch the captain's signals, bowlers back up the fieldsman, and so on.

'I remember walking out on to the Adelaide Oval and saying to someone, "What was that all about?"

'I got in reply, "Bazz, you will know, you will learn."'[26]

Queensland Test all-rounder Andy Bichel recalls one of his most treasured moments of his Test debut at Adelaide Oval in the 1990s: 'There were handshakes and pats on the back all-round, as is the case for a bloke playing his first Test. Nugget got on the table in the dressing-room and gave us a brilliant speech, then he got down off the table and grabbed my hand. He squeezed it really hard, gave me a wink and said, "Good luck today mate". It was as if he had played Test cricket himself and was passing on good advice to old and new about how to play this weird and wonderful game.'[27]

Nugget shed a tear or two the day Adam Gilchrist told him (in confidence) that he was about to hang up his gloves. 'Gilly is a great mate of mine and when he told me that he was going to retire on the Saturday before play started in the Test, I was pretty upset, but I knew he wanted to do it, because he's got a young family to think of—lovely family.'

But for Nugget and the players, there have been lots of fun times, too.

Dennis Lillee has always had a sense of fun which he brings to Adelaide Oval whenever he visits and catches up with Nugget. During the filming of *Australian Story*'s 'Man of the Century' in Perth, Lillee feigns a handshake with Nugget. As Nugget thrusts out his hand, Lillee goes to shake it, then at the last second he withdraws his hand. On other occasions he might grab Nugget's hat and throw it away in mock anger.

Lillee says: 'When Ian [Chappell] used to get Nugget onto the table in the dressing-room, Chappelli would load his gun, "What about the fielding, Nug?" and Nugget would say, "Yes, c'mon, get the fielding right." And I would pop up and say, "Hang on Nug, you know…"

'"Oh, no, you're okay, Dennis."

'Nugget's compassion and feeling for the cricketers makes you realise what a great human being he is and, you know, maybe some of us should have a bit more of that rather than just thinking of ourselves.'[28]

Once Nugget was asked if Doug Walters really did accompany him to a nightclub in Kings Cross. 'What happens on tour, stays on tour' is Nugget's stock answer.

Kookaburra boss Rob 'Super' Elliot teases Nugget that he heard of an incident on tour where Nugget had a shower with a young lady.

'Now Nugget,' Super would say, 'why did you share your shower with that girl?'

Quick as a flash, Nugget replies, 'To save water!'

Adam Gilchrist remembers Nugget coming to Melbourne with the Australian team for a one-day international: 'We all chipped in to have Nugget with us. We flew him over to Melbourne and had him stay at our hotel.

'He came out to training with us. Nugget was dressed in the team gear, full kit. I think he had the number 100 on his back. He wanted to join us in the warm-up. He wanted to do his stretches, so there he is doing a calf stretch and this and that, then we lie on our backs to do a certain stretch, then get up and run off to a position about 20 metres away. We look over and Nugget is still on the ground on his back. He was looking for help, he was a bit embarrassed, but too proud to call for help. It must have made interesting viewing for 80,000 people there that day at the MCG.

'Nugget keeps trying. It is extraordinary to see the lengths he goes to be a part of the team and to keep living his dream.'[29]

Nugget wasn't at The Oval in 1972 when Australia beat England on the sixth day of the final Test match. This game was very much a defining moment in modern Australian cricket history, for Ian Chappell's team had beaten a tough England unit led by Ray Illingworth. Both Ian and Greg Chappell scored Test centuries and Dennis Lillee grabbed 10 wickets for the match. There is an enduring image of Paul Sheahan (44 not out) and Rodney Marsh (43 not out) charging off the ground in the wake of Australia's 5-wicket victory, with Marsh whirling his bat. As the champagne and beer flowed in the Australian dressing-room, Marsh jumped onto a table and belted out, for the first time, the lines that would become a tradition for our Test men:

Under the Southern Cross I stand
A sprig of wattle in my hand
A native of my native land
Australia, you fuckin' beauty!

While Nugget wasn't present for the song's first airing, he's heard it countless times since. When Marsh retired, the team song was passed on to David Boon. Then Justin Langer sang it and Ricky Ponting. Now the sprig of wattle has been passed to Mike Hussey, the man Nugget calls 'Mr Cricketer'.

David Boon had a long reign—more than 100 Test matches—as the team's songster. Now manager of cricket operations for Tascricket and a Test selector, Boon says: 'Nugget is an amazing human being. He is considerate and passionate. I can recall on many occasions when players had been remiss and needed equipment such as batting grips or a jockstrap and Nugget would, with efficiency, rush to Rowe & Jarman's and procure the necessary items. He was a godsend. That's just the man.

'However, my fondest memories are of Nugget's pre-match speeches which he would give on the dressing-room table before we took the field. "Always keep your eye on the captain, walk in with the bowler, take your catches." He always spoke with authority and passion.

'Nugget is part of Australian cricket culture and as far as I am concerned so he should be.'[30]

Trevor Chappell, youngest of the famous three Chappell brothers, left SA in the 1970s to forge his career away from Adelaide, the family base. He later moved to Sydney to play for NSW and it was there that he really came into his own, making the 1981 Australian touring team to England. With great fondness, Trevor says: 'The main memories I have of Nugget are as "coach" of the SACA's basketball team for a couple of winters in the early 70s. He got on court in one game as a defender and did a great job, we even had trouble getting the ball from him.

'Another time we had won the premiership and were celebrating at some pub and a patron accidentally spilt some beer on a SACA blazer Nug was wearing and Nug was very upset with the fellow.

'The other thing I remember from the dressing-room is Nug being left stranded on the table in the middle of the room after giving one of his pep talks before we took the field. Once Nug had gotten up on the table, the players removed all the chairs so he couldn't get back down.'[31]

Neil 'Harpo' Marks saw the development of Nugget, the growth of his esteem and confidence. He got to know Nugget in the 1960s when he toured with the NSW team under Richie Benaud and Bob Simpson, and he met up with Nugget again during the 1980s when he went to Adelaide Oval with a NSW Sheffield Shield team. Over the years Harpo has also observed the effect that Nugget has on those around him. A great story-teller, Harpo says of Nugget:

'Sometimes in this crazy world there appears a person who is above it all; a person who really sees the forest and doesn't notice the scrubby bushes, the dirt and the quicksand. Strangely, it's not the Michelangelos, the Churchills or even the Sobers—it's the Nuggets. It has been an honour to know him. He's a man.'[32]

Nugget's special involvement with South Australian and Australian teams has continued unabated for all these years. Nugget is an Australian sporting legend—he wears the baggy-green cap proudly, he has a life-time Kookaburra equipment contract, he has scored more runs than any of the batting giants of cricket, including Don Bradman and W.G. Grace, and he has been friend, confidant and motivator to every first-class cricketer to have played at the Adelaide Oval over the past 45 years.

The players love Nugget. They embrace him, protect him and have helped give Nugget the chance to live his dreams. And while the players may be his heroes, they have a hero of their own: Barry 'Nugget' Rees—the Peter Pan of Australian cricket.

Notes

1   Tony McGuinness to author, June 2007
2   Wendy Page to author, Sydney, February 2008
3   Robert Joske at media conference, Steve Waugh's final Test match, SCG, 2004
4   *Out of my Comfort Zone*, Steve Waugh, Penguin Viking, Sydney, 2005, p. 720.
5   Darren Lehmann to author, July 2008
6   ibid.
7   ibid.
8   ibid.
9   ibid.
10   ibid.
11   ibid.
12   John Inverarity to author, 2007
13   Darren Lehmann to author, July 2008
14   ibid.
15   ibid.
16   ibid.
17   ibid.
18   ibid.
19   Neil Marks, *Tales for All Seasons*, Harper Sports, Harper Collins, Sydney, 1997 pp. 55–56
20   Phyllis Golding to author, August 2007
21   Dennis Lillee to author, November 2007
22   *Shane Warne, My Autobiography*, Shane Warne with Richard Hobson, Hodder & Stoughton, London, 2001, pp. 89–89
23   Darren Lehmann to author, July 2008
24   *Learning from Legends*, John Buchanan, LFL Media, Sydney, 2008
25   ibid.
26   Barry Curtin to author, May 2008
27   Andy Bichel in email to author, July 2008
28   Dennis Lillee to author, November 2007
29   Adam Gilchrist to author, 2008
30   David Boon in email to author, July 2008
31   Trevor Chappell in email to author, July 2008
32   Neil Marks in email to author, June 2008

CHAPTER 6

Nugget and AFL

Nugget's football adventure began all those years ago when he went to Alberton Oval with his father and Uncle Bill to watch their beloved Port Adelaide Magpies.

Port champion and Magpies and AFL Hall of Fame legend, Geof Motley remembers Nugget's presence at Alberton from around 1954. That very year Fos Williams coached the Magpies to his second premiership and that was the first of a golden run of five successive premierships. The 1954 premiership win was a fiercely fought exchange against West Adelaide, Williams' old team. At half-time the Magpies trailed by 25 points, but through 'high class and thrilling football'[1] they gradually gained the upper hand over the Bloods. At half-time every player on both sides was on Port's half-forward line throwing punches. There was a collision between Magpies centreman Dave Boyd and West's captain and centre-half-back Brian Faehse. Boyd was felled and the punch-up resulted. As the West Adelaide players left the field for half-time, a spectator in a black and white blazer charged through and punched Faehse on the jaw. Another spectator king-hit the attacker. But the Magpies came away with a 3-point victory.

The Rees household would have celebrated that night, but little could they have known that the 1954 flag was the beginning of a golden run and the start of the famous Williams dynasty. Fos Williams' charges won the 1954, 1955, 1956, 1957 and 1958 premierships and Nugget saw every one of those premiership wins.

The 1954 victory was, however, earned the hard way. The *Sunday Mail* newspaper summed it up in a page one headline: 'Ugly Melee at Oval Worst for 25 years'. West Adelaide chairman Jack Simmons told football writer Lawrie Jervis that the club lost the grand final because of the bashing players and officials got at half-time.

Bob McLean, a huge man in build and in deed, played football for Port and cricket for SA. An all-rounder, Big Bob played 16 Sheffield Shield matches for SA, scoring 863 runs at 34.52 with three centuries and a career high of 213. Delivering the slowest of slow gentle leg-breaks, McLean also claimed 52 wickets at an average of 39.

McLean was at the helm of the Port Adelaide administration the very year Port began to dominate AFL in

South Australia. From the outset Big Bob ran a tight ship at Alberton Oval. He quickly developed into one of the State's leading sports administrators and he brought his opponent (West Adelaide) to heel with this gem: 'A mobile wire fence is long overdue at the ovals. That has always been my feeling. I am not one of those who have laughed at this, but I have reached the stage where I can laugh at Mr Simmons' repeated excuses on how they lost the premiership. The winners can laugh. The losers can please themselves.'[2]

Barry Rees was a shade over ten years old when Port won the 1954 flag. He celebrated with a Coke and a pie (or was it two pies?) and then it was off home. Ray and Bill Rees celebrated the night in the company of the Port players and officials at a lavish premiership dinner at the Largs Pier Hotel. A huge mob turned up at the Alberton Oval clubrooms and a few days later a Premiership Ball was held at the Palais Royal. That season Roger Clift won the Magpies' fairest and best award, followed by Ted Whelan, Harold McDonald and Fos Williams. Lloyd Zucker won best player in the finals and Ken Tierney won best first year player. Laurie Stevens was the best utility and Neville 'Chicken' Hayes won an award for 'Most Attention to Training'.

In a referendum in 1967, the Australian people gave Aboriginal people the right to vote. It was a momentous occasion for all of Australia. In sport alone it meant greater acceptance for indigenous people in all walks of life, including football. It meant more indigenous players would grace our sports grounds in future. Already we had seen the magnificence of Graham 'Polly' Farmer, arguably the greatest footballer of them all. When Port Power was granted entry into the national competition in 1996, it meant Nugget would get to know many Aboriginal players who would remain firm friends. Nugget names Gavin Wanganeen, Byron Pickett, and Shaun and Peter Burgoyne, all AFL premiership players, among his mates.

In 1967 Bob McLean brought the Magpies a new club song. The song, which McLean 'stole' from South Melbourne, is the one now sung by the Sydney Swans. But Bob McLean changed a few words to suit the Magpies:

Cheer, cheer the black and the white
Honour the Magpie by day and by night
Lift that loyal banner high
Shake down the thunder from the sky
Whether the odds be great or be small
We'll come out and win overall
While our players keep on fighting
Onward to victory

How often Nugget has joined in to sing the club song alongside the players, his heroes.

It was the rough, tough 1954 premiership match with West Adelaide which may have brought the Magpies their reputation as a bunch of street-fighters on the field. Fos Williams went on to coach Port to nine premierships: 1954, 1955, 1956, 1957, 1958, 1962, 1963 and 1965. Geof Motley, the man Nugget always used to address as 'Geoffrey Motley, number 17', coached Port to the 1959 premiership and then Sturt, under the guidance of another super coach, Jack Oatley, began a dynasty of his own, winning the flag six times on the trot.

In 1974 the South Australian Cricket Association (SACA) and the South Australian National Football League (SANFL) came to loggerheads. Two men of the most stubborn disposition—the SACA's president Sir Donald Bradman and the SANFL's president Judge Don Brebner—could not agree on a range of issues until eventually the SANFL decided to take their ball and go to a new venue, away from Adelaide Oval.

Nugget was sad about the break for he had a foot in both camps. He was, by 1974, something of a legend in South Australian cricket and he was also inextricably linked to the Magpies. Adelaide Oval was his Mecca.

Bob McLean was quoted in *The News* (the now defunct Adelaide afternoon tabloid newspaper) on the eve of the 1975 preliminary final as saying, 'You football writers never learn. You're too busy mixing it with the aristocrats at Unley, the bluebloods at Norwood and the nobs at the Bay. You want to come down to Alberton and slum it with the workers like us. I've told you before—stick with Port Adelaide and you'll win a lot more than you lose.'[3]

McLean was being light-hearted, but beneath the façade was an intense feeling of pride for his club. The Magpies kept a lid on things. As McLean once said, 'No one finds out anything we don't want them to know.'[4] The spirit of Big Bob remains with Port. They like the winning habit.

Port lost the 1976 Grand Final at Football Park under coach Jack Cahill, but over the following 19 seasons Cahill coached the Magpies to an incredible 10 flags: 1977, 1979, 1980, 1981, 1988, 1989, 1990, 1992, 1995 and 1996. Cahill won three successive flags (1979–81) then he left Port for a period of five years to play two seasons with Collingwood and three with West Adelaide. He returned to the Magpies in 1988, and guided his men to the 1988 flag.

Cahill said, 'Port supporters have a lot to do with the club always being competitive. They are like the Collingwood fans. They demand success.'[5]

Through all the years, victorious or otherwise, Nugget waved the Magpies colours. All clubs have their red-hot supporters, but Nugget was the hottest of the hot. The players got to know him well and trusted him, so too the officials and the other fans. Nugget seemed to know everyone, the players, their wives and girlfriends, the players' children.

He has known most of the Port Adelaide Hall of Fame inductees, including Jeff Potter, Geof Motley, John Abley, David Boyd, Foster Williams, Ted Whelan and Bob McLean among the old guard, and the likes of Russell Ebert, Scott Hodges, Tim Evans, Greg Phillips, Brian Cunningham, Craig Bradley, Tim Ginever, Harry Kneebone, Richard Russell and Darren Smith. Nugget held every player in the highest esteem, regardless of what grade they played in. He encouraged them all.

Nugget used to call in and see Geof Motley and Russell Ebert at their workplace. He kicked the football with Neville 'Chicken' Hayes and other workmates such as Russell Moyle, Arthur 'Slugger' Slee and John Papandrea in Chesser Street, the little laneway next to Rowe & Jarman's store fronting Grenfell Street.

In the early 1980s Nugget found himself team manager for Walkerville Under-12s. The team included his nephews, Hamish and Cameron Freeman (Pam's sons)—the team's wingers—and rover Corey Smith (Diane's son); centreman Josh Francou; ruckman Ben Holland; and centre-half-forward Nick Holland. Nugget remembers their skill at a young age: 'We had a good side and the boys were really good, winning two premierships and one runners-up trophy in three years.

'Of course Josh and Ben and Nick went on to become AFL champions. Josh starred for Port Power and we still keep in touch.'

Josh Francou writes for a Sunday newspaper and works for Radio 5AA as special comments man at AFL matches. He is not afraid of telling it as he sees it. Francou was only seven or eight years old when Nugget managed Walkerville.

'I can't remember much about Nugget then,' Francou says. 'But I got to know him when I was at the Power.

'What a lovely bloke. He is the most loyal, trustworthy person you'll ever meet. He never has a bad word to say about anyone. And Nugget has a good sense of humour, ever smiling and always positive.

'Even if I only got one kick and one handball, having a terrible time of it, Nugget would tell me how well I played. Sometimes he used to drop in to see my wife and me when we lived in Henley Beach, and I remember him telling me so many stories as I drove him home after training. Nugget is a sheer delight.'[6]

Port Adelaide has always been Nugget's passion and it was a sad day in 1990 when Port was edged out of contention to join the AFL. There has always been a 'them and us' attitude towards Port from the rest of the SANFL clubs, but when Port tried to get in first to the AFL the resistance was near paranoia. In his book *From Port to a Power*, Bruce Abernethy wrote: 'If a single club was chosen to join the AFL, then all logic pointed to it being Port Adelaide. But unanimous agreement among a ten-team league about which club should join the party would have been like achieving world peace. There was a real war going on in Kuwait. People were fighting for their lives, but the drama was overshadowed in all areas of the South Australian media by the Port Adelaide announcement.'[7]

Port Adelaide Magpies President Bruce Weber had told the football world that the Magpies had signed a deal with the

AFL as the next team into the national competition. That's when all the other clubs banded together to exclude Port. Some six weeks later the Magpies scooped the pool at the Magarey Medal function, a night held in the middle of the finals series. Port's Scott Hodges won the Magarey Medal and the leading goal-kicking award; Simon Tregenza came second in the Medal; Troy Bond won the Seconds Magarey Medal; and standing among the trophy winners Weber yelled, 'We came, collected the hardware and now we're going home!'[8]

Port's opponents have never relished the Magpies' confidence. Many called it arrogance, but the spirit stemmed from a long history of winning. The 1990 flag was Jack Cahill's seventh premiership as coach, and his third flag in a row since returning to Alberton. Logically, SA needed to opt for one of the two most successful clubs in the SANFL—Port Adelaide or Norwood. In the end it was neither club. Instead a hastily put-together collection of players from all clubs was selected and in late October 1990, the Adelaide Football Club's first list was named.

Graham Cornes was given the coaching role and there were ten Port Adelaide stars in the 57 names on that initial list. They were David Brown, George Fiacchi, Scott Hodges, David Hutton, Russel Johnston, Greg Phillips, Darren Smith, Stephen Williams and Bruce Abernethy. On December 21, 1990, Greg Phillips quit the club and six days later Stephen Williams followed suit.

The 1990 premiership cut deep for Glenelg, in particular

Graham Cornes, the Glenelg coach, who said candidly to the jubilant Port players and officials after the grand final that while Glenelg had the better playing list, 'Port won and I give credit to their competitiveness'.[9]

While Port won the flag, Cornes, as expected, won the Crows coaching job over Jack Cahill, who was well on his way to becoming the most successful SANFL coach of all time. With the Crows now in the AFL, Nugget was in a bit of a quandary.

Nugget had dearly wanted to follow Port into the big league, but they were pipped at the post. So, until Port belatedly won an AFL license in 1996, Nugget followed the Crows. He doesn't talk much about it these days—in fact he refuses to talk about it—but there are some that don't let him forget.

His good mate Tony 'Freddie' McGuinness, former Crows captain and now forwards coach for Port Power, hardly lets Nugget forget his time barracking for the Crows. McGuinness first got to know Nugget when he joined Rowe & Jarman as a salesman in 1985. He was a champion footballer with Glenelg in the SANFL, and in 1986 McGuinness joined the Western Bulldogs. After a brilliant stint with the Bulldogs, McGuinness returned to Adelaide as a partner with Rowe & Jarman and a key recruit of the Adelaide Football Club.

McGuinness says: 'I got to know Nugget at the shop before I went to Victoria. We'd go to have coffee and I, like everyone else, found I warmed to him immediately.

'I have always taken him on face value. Here was this terribly friendly and genuine person wanting to engage in a conversation. And that is a hard thing not to do with Nugget. I guess I embraced the relationship pretty well as much as everybody does and we formed a very strong friendship.

'We'd go to lunch and even though Nugget barracked for Port, he started to follow Glenelg a bit. Well, Glenelg became his second team. I went to the cricket with him a couple of times. It was after I came back from Victoria that I got to know him better. He is now part of our family, as he is with others. Nugget has many "families".'[10]

After Port Adelaide's abortive attempt to be the first South Australian team in the AFL, McGuinness and former Rowe & Jarman employee Chris McDermott, who had been a champion Glenelg footballer and was the Crows captain, 'worked' on Nugget to show allegiance to the Adelaide Football Club. Nugget would accompany the Crows playing group for 'away' matches.

McGuinness recalls how Nugget would revel in the opportunity to mix with his football heroes: 'It is a big day for him. He gets the plane over and he is in the rooms before the game, spending a bit of time there at half-time and then at the end of the game. Win, lose or draw Nugget is in the rooms, sometimes consoling or celebrating, but always encouraging the players. If the side loses, according to Nugget's Law a loss is still a win, for not getting the points was someone's else's fault—never the players for whom he is so super-loyal.

'Nugget would come to Crows training with Chris [McDermott] or me. The Crows experience gave him a new lease of life.'[11]

It was Tony McGuinness and Chris McDermott who later teamed to form the McGuinness-McDermott Foundation, raising money for underprivileged and sick children.

When Port Adelaide finally started playing in the AFL in 1997, Nugget changed his allegiance to the new Port Power because they were an extension of the Port Magpies, the team he, his father Ray and his uncle Bill adored.

In the year of 1997 Nugget was seen wearing a unique scarf: one side the colours of Port Power, the other side Adelaide Crows.

If he had a foot in both camps, that was soon rectified.

Nugget might have walked for a time in the Crows' shoes, but you can bet he wore a pair of Magpies socks. His love for Port Adelaide never waned.

Much to Nugget's and every Port supporter's delight, the Port Adelaide Football Club won the second license for an SA club to go into the AFL. Port became the AFL's 17th team and permission came on May 21, 1996, although it took until June 4 for the AFL to ratify the deal.

Port did not start playing in the AFL until the 1997 season, but a year earlier the club had already pledged John Cahill to be Port's first coach in the AFL. On June 22, 1996, Cahill coached his Magpies for the final time, handing over to Stephen Williams, Mark's brother. Port again won the grand final, a premiership flag to both Cahill and Williams. For Cahill it was his tenth flag as coach.

But he was more intent upon making things work for the Power.

Nugget was pleased overall, but he had the odd issue— like Simon Tregenza, the great Port Magpies player, getting picked up by the Crows. Then another one 'got away': Norwood's Tom Harley played just one match with the Power, then he moved to Geelong where he has dominated in the backlines for the Cats, become captain of the club and led his team to premiership glory in the 2007 grand final— against Nug's beloved Port Power.

Back in 1997, Essendon coach Kevin Sheedy, who was fully aware of Port's great winning ways, warned the football community: 'The AFL doesn't realise what it is doing allowing Port Adelaide into the competition.'[12]

Port Power's first list excited Port fans, for there were enough champion Magpies to whet their appetites. The first list was: Gavin Wanganeen (Essendon); Shayne Brewer (Eagles, SA); Matthew Primus (Geelong); Ian Downsborough (West Perth); Shane Bond (Port Adelaide); Fabian Francis (Melbourne); Scott Cummings (Essendon); Brayden Lyle (Port Adelaide); John Rombotis (Fitzroy); Josh Francou (North Adelaide); Steven Paxman (Fitzroy); Brent Heaver (Melbourne); Warren Tredrea (Port Adelaide); Jonathon Yebury (Norwood); Nigel Fiegert (Port Adelaide); David Brown (Port Adelaide); Mark Harwood (Tassie Mariners);

Bowen Lockwood (Geelong Falcons); Donald Dickie (Norwood); Scott Matthews (Woodville-West Torrens); Brendon Lade (South Adelaide); Damien Squires (North Adelaide); Stephen Daniels (Norwood); Nathan Eagleton (West Adelaide); Adam Kingsley (Essendon); Peter Burgoyne (Port Adelaide); Darryl Poole (Port Adelaide); Tom Harley (Norwood); Paul Geisler (North Melbourne); Nathan Steinberner (Central District); Scott Freeborne (Woodville-West Torrens); Mark Conway (Port Adelaide); Darren Mead (Port Adelaide); Stephen Carter (Port Adelaide); Stuart Dew (Central District); Paul Evans (Port Adelaide); Roger James (Norwood); Jake Lynch (Woodville-West Torrens); Adam Heuskes (Norwood); Tom Carr (Port Adelaide); Andrew Osborne (South Adelaide); Scott Bassett (Norwood); Jarrad Cotton (North Adelaide); and Rhett Biglands (Woodville-West Torrens).

In the AFL Port Adelaide had to forego its traditional black and white jumper and its Magpie emblem because of the obvious clash with the already established AFL side, Collingwood.

On March 29, 1997, Port Power played its first AFL match against Collingwood, before 51,000 fans at the MCG. At the end of the home and away season, Port finished just 2 points out of the finals race, finishing ninth in what was described as a brilliant first-up attempt.

In 1997 the Crows made history winning the first of two flags on the trot by beating St Kilda in the grand final. A week after Malcolm Blight's Crows beat the Saints, Nugget watched his Port Magpies win the 1997 SANFL grand final, the second flag to Stephen Williams.

The Magpies won again in 1999, the most recent Magpies SANFL premiership.

While Nugget had seen great changes in the Port Magpies, there were also changes afoot at Rowe & Jarman. In 1996 Dennis Sims and silent partner Tony McGuinness bought the store from Ed Betro.

Uncharacteristically, Nugget didn't enjoy his last few years with the firm as he did with the first 40 years, and he finally gave it away in 2002. Nugget said he quit 'because of the stress', but he wouldn't elaborate.

Friends rallied around. Nugget did some PR work for the McGuiness-McDermott Foundation and there were fund-raisers, such as the famous 'A Night with Nugget' in 2003.

It was at that event that McGuinness and a legion of Nugget Rees fans realised how far he had come in terms of self-confidence and his ability to 'work' an audience. McGuinness says: 'Nugget was quicker on the re-bound than compere James Brayshaw, and speakers Merv Hughes, Steve Waugh, Ian Chappell and David Hookes that night. These guys were all experienced and smart speakers. Nugget out did the lot of them.'[13]

In June 2006, Nugget received an offer of employment from Parkinson and Blunden. Sam Parkinson had known Nugget for years. Sam's father, Dave, or DH, as he is affectionately known, ran a sports manufacturing agency and he got to know Nugget very well, along with all the Rowe & Jarman staff.

All within Adelaide sporting goods firms knew of Nugget's stress in not having a job. So the Parkinsons decided to do something about it. Nugget was offered a job, just one day a week, but the job gave Nug a new lease on his working life.

PARKINSON BLUNDEN

115 Rundle Street

Kent Town SA 5067

Friday, June 23, 2006

Dear Mr Rees,

Or can I call you Nugget?

It gives me great pleasure to formally offer you a position with our company at Parkinson Blunden.

We propose that your hours are approximately 11am–1.30pm on each and every Thursday. You will report to Mr. Hans Ellenbroek, who is also a newcomer, who will report to Mr. Terry Blunden, who will report to me!

In addition to your working contract, I will need to discuss your on-field requirements, in consultation with Mr. Elliot from Kookaburra Sport. I trust that you will accept this offer and I look forward to working with you in the near future.

Yours sincerely.

(Signed)

Sam Parkinson

Thursday with Nugget is something else. His great mate from Goodwood Saints Football Club, Tiny Nelson, picks him up at his Colonel Light Gardens home at about 9.30 a.m. Tiny drives Nugget to a cafe in Halifax Street, Adelaide, for coffee. Those who have got to know Nugget through getting their coffee at this cafe are often there to greet Nug on a Thursday. It is a special time. Nugget is the centre of attention, but his attention is always focused on the person to whom he is speaking.

Frequently David Rowe and Barry Jarman arrive to say hello. Nugget is never far from their protective radar. An hour or so later, if Tiny can drag Nugget away from the cafe, the lengthy farewells are done and they set off for Kent Town and Nugget's work day at Parkinson Blunden, which is now called Sam Parkinson Marketing.

Faces light up the instant Nugget walks through the front doors. Sam Parkinson is often there to greet him, along with DH (Dave Parkinson) and Terry Blunden. Nugget shakes hands all round, then ducks out into the warehouse where he meets up with his old mate, Hans Ellenbroek.

Hans makes Nugget a cup of coffee ('no sugar please', he has his own little container of sugar-free sweeteners) and the pair chat like there is no tomorrow. Coffee done, Nugget joins Terry Blunden and the pair do their 'rounds' of the various manufacturers' agencies. Terry Blunden is semi-retired, but he always looks forward to Thursdays with Nugget. Blunden says, 'This man is a very special person and Thursdays I never miss. It is just a brilliant two hours for me to spend with Nug. Spending time with Nug makes my week.'[14]

When they return, Hans and Nug go to the Alma Hotel for some well-earned R & R. Nugget has a schnitzel and a Coke Zero. Hans has a beer with his lunch, but he is more intent upon placing a bet on the horses or the dogs. Theirs is a special bond.

Having worked for D.H. Parkinson for 18 years, Hans Ellenbroek decided he needed a change of scenery. He joined the department store Harris Scarfe for a time, before moving to Rowe & Jarman as a salesman in 1984. Later Hans was employed by Sam Parkinson (DH's son) at Parkinson Blunden. He had known Nugget for years, but at the shop he got to know him better. So well, in fact, that Hans, a good amateur league footballer, introduced Nugget to the Saints.

Since then, every Thursday Nugget has been tripping along to Goodwood Saints Football Club training with Hans. There Hans is the club's head trainer and Nugget has risen through the ranks to become assistant trainer.

While writing this book, I attended Saints training to see Nugget going about his business.

Hans explains: 'Nugget's job every Thursday night is to greet the people—every single one of them. He always says "Hello" to every person. He puts his gear, scarf, cap or beanie, and bag, in the same corner and places his coat on the back of a chair, same chair. Nugget sorts the football betting tip sheets and places them in the dining room. Then he helps me prepare. He puts on his medical bag—it's not unlike one of those money belts—and loads up on tape and Dencorub.'[15]

Nugget then checks on the juniors. He talks to everyone, the players, the wives and girlfriends, the children. He asks the youngsters whether they have any niggles. Nugget is dying to give someone a rub-down. Hans says watching Nugget massage a player is worth seeing: 'Nug squeezes out almost the entire tube of Dencorub and it takes at least half an hour to get the stuff off the player.'[16]

Hans always tries to have Nugget walk a couple of laps. He might be walking with a youngster recovering from a hamstring injury or 'general soreness', a common footballer's complaint. The walk is always a boon to any youngster, for they get to spend quality time with him, and it helps Nugget to shed the odd pound.

The 2008 Goodwood Saints captain, Charlie Thomas, describes Nugget as a 'man of incredible wisdom and character'. Thomas says: 'He surprises me every time I meet him. He sums up people brilliantly without being judgemental, he is very perceptive. Nugget also has the best collection of clichés you've ever seen, but he never uses the same cliché twice. He has been fantastic with my whole family. He treats everyone the same—with respect.'[17]

The Goodwood Saints Football Club's No. 1 ticket holder, Nugget stood to speak. He took the microphone with the same self-assurance that he has always displayed with a cricket bat in his hand. And he spoke with affection and great humour. It was the night before we ventured down to Allberton Oval to speak with Mark Williams, Port Power coach. 'Rowdy and I are going to Alberton Oval tomorrow, to speak to some of the Power boys and Choco [Williams], and before that we are going to see Matthew Richardson at the Magpies...'

'Now that will be enough of that, Fat Boy,' says Hans Ellenbroek with mock dissention.

Nugget fires off one-liners like a comic professional. At the time he was spending a couple of days at his niece's flat, looking after her pets while she was away. 'I'm staying at my niece Cassie's place. Very good. No-one else around, only a little cat, no-one else around, no girls. That's the only thing I'm missing. And Hans wants a girl too. Thanks very much, much.'

He brings the house down, but the laughter that resounds around the Goodwood Saints Football Club is a collective show of deep love and affection for the man.

Saints player David Bartel says that Nugget always brings a smile to his face. 'It doesn't matter whether you are an A-grade player or a run-of-the-mill C-grader, Nugget treats you the same—always with total respect and loyalty.'[18]

The next day we were off to Alberton Oval to interview the Port Power players. We turned up for lunch and Nugget knew everyone in the lunch room. There were a few Port players sitting with coaching and other football club staffers and Nugget walked straight up to Warren Tredrea and thumped him on the back. Port had begun the season badly—four losses in a row—but Nugget was typically upbeat: 'You'll be right Tredders, kick goals not points, we'll be right. Port will win on Saturday.'

Nugget went through the list of players he felt we needed to speak with—a list of 24. I explained that it wasn't practical in the time available, but his philosophy was that if we interview one person, we had to talk to them all, because the players we don't speak to might 'get a bit hurt and upset'.

We had a drink with Barry Curtin, the dining room manager and PR man at the club, and he mentioned that it would be good if we could turn up at Maughan Thiem Ford in Cheltenham. We decided to go there before the Port Power training. Nugget had his schnitzel, I had fish and chips. 'Grilled, not battered fish, Rowdy,' Nugget smiled, wagging his right index finger at me.

Mike Perry greeted us at Maughan Thiem Ford and took us immediately to the Celebrity White Board in the showroom's sales office. Amongst the many signatures was one from Chopper Read, with the little rider, 'Never Plead Guilty!' Nugget and I both signed the board, but we had to keep moving—we had a lot of interviews ahead if Nugget got his way.

When a football team is heading into game number five after four defeats in a row, you'd expect the atmosphere to be a bit bleak. In fact the Port players were a bit down—until they set eyes on Nugget. He waltzed into the meeting room and slapped blokes on the back. 'C'mon Rowdy,' he called, 'they are waiting to start the meeting.'

Coach Mark Williams talked to the players about my writing a book on Nugget. It was immediately clear that all the coaches and players love Nugget and, as Wendy Page found with Australian cricketers when filming 'Man of the Century', they were genuinely eager to be involved in a Nugget story.

One of the AFL's most accomplished 'taggers' Kane Cornes, the man who shut down the Brisbane Lions play-maker Simon Black to help Port Power win its first premiership in 2004, spoke lovingly about Nugget: 'I was about 14 years old when I started doing a bit of part-time work with Rowe & Jarman. The players love him. Even when he's not here, we often talk about his joyous spirit and positive outlook. His little sayings, like mispronouncing the dish "Chicken Farmer Jarmer", his handshakes—but the main thing is his big smile. There have been some funny things, of course, such as when Choco gets him on the table to address the team. He brings joy to the players.'[19]

The skilful left-footed half-forward Brett Ebert talks with relish about the day Nugget gave him a 'Goodwood Saints-style chop-suey massage'. 'Thanks to Nugget's great massage

I started to catch the ball within range and kick a few goals. When I need a boost I think about Nugget kicking a few balls to me.'[20]

The ex-North Melbourne and Port Power player, now players' welfare officer, Stewart Cochrane got to know Nugget through mates such as Roger James and Josh Francou, 'who told me about this ripper bloke'. Cochrane says: 'Nugget always has a good word for everyone. He always makes you feel good. When you talk to Nugget, whether it's for five minutes or fifteen, you forget your troubles. You just enjoy the time with him.'

Cochrane recalls an occasion when he and good mate Stuart Dew, the 2004 Port premiership player now with Hawthorn, drove Nugget home after a Port loss. 'Nugget was in the back seat and we were a bit down after the Port loss. Nugget asked Stu how his girlfriend was?

'"Actually, Nug, we've broken up," Stu said.

'Quick as a flash Nugget replied, "Can I have her phone number? She's a lovely girl. I want to make sure she is alright." Nugget is a beauty!'[21]

Playing for Central District in the SANFL and working in the Police Credit Union in town, the young Stuart Dew got to know Nugget Rees long before he began playing for Port Power. Dew says, 'I immediately liked the bloke. Then when I went to the Power he often had the group in stitches in the dressing-room, or delivering a pre-game pep-talk. I remember he used to always say, "Now c'mon you fellas, goals not points" and when he uttered those words he looked straight at Tredders [Port Power captain Warren Tredrea].'[22]

Dew recalls one of his favourite Nugget moments: 'One day at AAMI Stadium Nug was watching us train. He was doing what he usually did, walking around the boundary. We were doing some up and down the ground work when we called him on to the field to join in. So there he was with his Port scarf on and he snuck into the forward pocket just as the ball came in. He took a chest mark, and he wasn't quite sure what to do, so I yelled, "Over to me Nug" and he gave off a slick handball and we finished that little drill without missing a beat. It was always a thrill to get him involved on the field. Good for Nugget and very special for all of the players.'[23]

Another great moment is a photo of Nugget and Dew taken in the lounge bar of the Hyde Park Tavern in Adelaide, which Dew co-owns with Warren Tredrea and Chad Cornes. He and Nugget had swapped sports gear so Dew was wearing Nugget's 1964 Test baggy-green and an Australian Test match shirt with player number 370, while Nug was in Dew's 2004 Port Power Premiership jumper.

Stuart Dew dropped out of AFL football for a season, then was picked up by Hawthorn in time for the 2008 season. Nugget, Dew says, isn't happy about the move. 'Nugget still rings me. He rings and says, "Now Stuey, when are you coming back to Port? We'll have you back, we need you." Every week at least, I hear from Nug and he always tries to convince me to return.'[24]

As it has turned out, Port Power's 2008 season was in direct contrast to Hawthorn. The Hawks have proved a genuine premiership contender and Dew played a starring role with his long, raking drop punts into the Hawthorn forward line. Midway through the 2008 season Hawthorn played the Adelaide Crows at AAMI Stadium and Dew was keen to have Nugget down in the rooms before the match. He says, 'I'd told the boys all about Nugget and they were keen to have him give us a pep-talk. But Nug couldn't make it. However, I will get him to one of our matches and I'll get him to wear the Hawks jumper and to give us a rousing talk.'

Dew had one reservation, however: 'I reckon he'll agree to wear our Hawthorn jumper in the rooms, but I reckon he'll still be wearing his Port Power scarf.'[25]

Port skipper Warren Tredrea spoke of the players 'feeding on Nugget's positive mood'. 'One day at training we had Nugget running about in a Power guernsey,' Tredrea says. 'He adds that little bit to make our footy club unique.'[26]

Tough-nut backman Stephen Salopek says, 'Nugget is the best character at the club. He exudes a passion that we all enjoy. Doesn't matter who you are, the star player at Port, a rookie or the boot-studder, he treats everyone the same. We embrace Nugget with our arms wide open. He brings out the best in people.'[27]

Chad Cornes has known Nugget for a large part of his life. Cornes and his brother Kane got a job at Rowe & Jarman through their family connection with Tony McGuinness. Their father Graham Cornes, former SANFL and North Melbourne player, played alongside McGuinness at Glenelg. Cornes says, 'I was about 11 or 12 when I met Nug. We've been good mates ever since. No matter how bad you're feeling, when you see Nug you cheer up. In 2006 we had lost five games in a row, so the coach got Nugget to give us a pump-up speech. Not many people get to speak to the group. Certainly Nugget gets that opportunity.'[28]

Defender Jacob Surjen says: 'The first time I met Nugget was in 2004 when we won the grand final. Nugget came to training every Wednesday night and introduced himself and we've been good mates ever since. Before every game there's always a call from the great man lending his support and wishing us luck. After a win, Nugget always rings and leaves a great message of about three minutes. It's great. We love him. He's a champion.'[29]

By this time, we'd spoken to most of the Port players, but according to Nugget there were a lot more. 'I don't want anyone to get upset that we didn't give them a chance to say something,' he said. I explained, again, that we weren't compiling a telephone directory and he laughed and gave me a double thumbs up. We agreed that we'd talk to a few of the more younger players before moving on to the coaches.

Brendon Lade says Nugget 'would do anything for you. He has a lovely nature and never has a bad word to say about anyone. We are protective of Nugget and once the players get to know him, they love him.'[30]

'He's a joy to be around,' Dean Brogan says. 'Initially I thought, "Who's this bloke?" but then I discovered his specialness. There is an aura about Nugget. He is respected by everyone, the players, coaches, the fans, young or old. Nugget is a special friend.'

Brogan has often given Nugget a lift home from training. 'Nugget always knows the way, "Your side, my side".' (This was something I experienced when I finally dragged him away from Alberton Oval and set out for his home. Nugget doesn't know the road names too well, but he directs you precisely all the way. 'Straight ahead and my side, then your side, my side, your side.' 'My side' means turn left, and 'your side' means turn right. Simple.)

Brogan also has great respect for Nugget's family, especially his sister, Di. 'They are a very close family. Very loving.'[31]

Michael Wilson was just coming back from serious injury when we spoke about Nugget: 'Nugget's been around at the club for as long as I can remember. Footy clubs can be stressed-out places, so Nug lightens the mood and he always puts a smile on the faces of everyone down here. He's a good, honest bloke. And he's smart. I saw his business card and I haven't seen so many letters after someone's name for a long time.'[32]

Power half-back, Michael Pettigrew hails from Western Australia. He recalls: 'I met Nugget some five years ago. During those first few weeks I was in Adelaide, Nugget was so welcoming and helped me through those inevitable periods of homesickness. He was terrific for a young bloke coming to a club interstate. Nugget is top of the tree as far as characters go.'[33]

After our Alberton Oval visit, Port Power won their next two matches.

The next time Nugget took me down to Alberton we caught up with the Power coach, Mark 'Choco' Williams. Mark is the son of Port Magpies legend Fos Williams and brother of Anthony, who was tragically killed in an accident, and Stephen, a Port Magpies player and three times premiership coach. Mark Williams played with the Port Magpies, then Collingwood, then Brisbane, and he coached Glenelg and was assistant coach to Kevin Sheedy at Essendon before he took over from Jack Cahill at the Power.

Williams recalls: 'I guess I first got to know Nugget about six years ago. Tony McGuinness used to bring him down to training. Nugget was always around the place in winter, although you wouldn't see him at all in the summer.

'One day I kidded him about being a Crows supporter and there he was rummaging through his bag getting out all his Port gear like a man on a mission searching for his union card.

'Nugget has an interesting insight into everything. I guess he got closer to our playing group through his association with Tony [McGuinness] and Chad and Kane [Cornes]. At Essendon Sheedy used to encourage a couple of fanatical supporters—blokes we called the Phantom and Rain Man—and I guess that experience along with Tony's enthusiasm for Nugget taught me a bit as well.

'If we can add a bit of joy and sparkle to his life, why not?'[34]

Initially Williams had no idea of Nugget's special relationship with the South Australian and Australian cricket teams—until Wendy Page's *Australian Story* 'Man of the Century' hit our television screens in January 2007.

'I was unaware of the top cricket connection,' Williams says. 'All I knew was Nugget was a special person. He had special attributes that would win us all over. He is the most positive guy. But he's also smart—Nugget can sense the mood. If you're down, he can be understanding of it. He keeps quiet at the appropriate time. He is respectful of different situations.

'Nugget always lightens the mood whether things are tight, we are in a form slump or doing okay. He'll change the mood of everyone and he gives us a touch of reality. We'd say, "Bloody hell, you're feeling bad. Have a look how this guy can get on with life and enjoy himself."'[35]

In the winter of 2006, Port had lost four games in a row, so Williams got Nugget in to analyse the training session. A man who listens and absorbs information like a human sponge, Nugget had picked up all the usual football clichés, of which there are many, along with the odd snippet from radio and television commentaries. He had also listened to the Power forwards coach, Tony McGuinness, who has what Williams calls 'a different jargon, which is only understood by his forwards. Any outsider would be thinking, "What the hell's he talking about?"'[36]

Armed with a truckload of football sayings, plus his own special brand of describing things, Nugget stood before the coach and the AFL players.

Williams continues: 'He didn't always get the names or the drills right, but the session with Nugget was hilarious. He hates people kicking points and usually says, "Kick goals, not points", but this time he had it the wrong way round and said "Kick points, not goals". When we pointed that out to him, he roared laughing and we laughed with him. He gives us a stream of jokes—it's enlightening. It's fantastic.'[37]

Having known him for a few years and now aware of his contact with the Australian cricket team, Williams, who had noticed that Nugget was always getting players to autograph a variety of merchandise to give to charities, asked if Nugget could get something signed for his sons, who were into cricket.

Williams had forgotten the request until Nugget arrived at Alberton Oval just prior to the start of the 2008 AFL season.

'I hadn't seen Nugget for months,' Williams says. 'During the cricket season he disappears. Nugget came into our dressing-room, greeted all the players as usual, then I noticed him delve into his bag. He came up with two glowing white cricket balls.

'I had a look at one of the balls. I couldn't recognise the signatures. "Who's this mate?"

'"Oh, one of the players," Nugget replied.

'Turned out to be Andrew Symonds. One of my boys is a real Symonds fans, along with thousands of other kids throughout Australia.

'The other ball was signed by Mitchell Johnson. It so happens that Mitchell Johnson is my other lad's favourite cricketer.

'Those two cricket balls Nugget got for me were like pots of gold to my kids.'[38]

Williams sees the 'joy' Nugget gets from 'being around the guys' but it works the other way too. 'When he turns up for lunch at Alberton Oval, all the coaches invite him over to join them. They love his company, as indeed we all do.

'Nugget is brilliant too with the young blokes, just as he is with players of all ages and stages in their careers.

'He is a great example to humanity. He keeps us at the footy club in touch with reality. He teaches us how people should be treated. Nugget is a good lesson for us all.'[39]

Former Essendon and Port Adelaide defender-mid-fielder Adam Kingsley, now Port Power's backline coach, started with the club in 1997. He says: 'Coming across from Melbourne I didn't realise the personality Nugget was and just how much impact he had on the players. Who is this guy they are all talking to with such enthusiasm? There were a couple of guys at Essendon, like the Phantom, and I guess Choco [Williams] is a bit like Sheeds [Kevin Sheedy] here, giving people a go. You meet Nugget and you realise what a great personality he has.'[40]

Former champion ruckman, now Port Power assistant coach, Matthew Primus recalls: 'I first saw Nugget when Freddy [Tony McGuinness] brought him to the club. I'd heard about Nugget's links with the Redbacks and the Australian cricket team and I think he had a bit of Crows blood in him, but we soon had him turn towards us. I think those few years we were winning got Nugget our way. But regardless if we win, lose or draw Nugget is great support. With our situation at the moment, we are not travelling too well, but he's here with a smile on his face. Guys who are living footy day in day out, they get to see Nugget with a smile on his face, they get to realise that "Hey, it's another day, let's move on". Nugget also comes into my pub [Hyde Park Tavern] and talks to every person in the bar—he keeps 'em in there.'[41]

In the old days, players from all the other clubs used to dread driving past the Cheltenham cemetery, for just ahead lay the fearsome Port Magpies. There was no fear for

Nugget as we scuttled past the cemetery on the way to the Port Magpies administrative offices. Nugget confidently strolled in and I tagged along. He knew all the staff and politely asked for the Chief Executive Officer, Matthew Richardson. Richardson knew Nugget from the days when he played for Kensington Cricket Club. He was relatively new in the job at the Magpies after a seven-year stint with the South Australian Cricket Association.

Matthew spoke of the Magpies thirst for success. 'What really hit me when I came here was the hunger to win flags,' he says. 'That's the big difference between the attitude here and at Adelaide Oval. The SACA doesn't seem to care whether they win or lose. Here it is life and death. A lot of the old guard won't countenance anything but a premiership. In the old days, Alberton Oval used to host some 20,000 people of a Saturday.'[42]

That was a little dig at the SACA's attitude.

I looked over at Nugget.

He was quiet.

The Port Magpies weren't winning too often at that point in the season and the SACA had just finished another dreadful year.

Nugget said confidently, 'The Magpies will come good—and so will the Redbacks.'

Matthew then extolled the virtues of one Barry 'Nugget' Rees: 'There is an aura about Nugget. To meet him is fantastic. Doesn't matter whether Nugget is with the Browns

[Kensington], the Port Magpies, the Goodwood Saints, Port Power, the Redbacks or the Australian cricket team, he is still the same bloke. I see Nugget with the Test players and he is exactly the same with them as he is with us at the Browns.'[43]

At a Magpies fundraising function, Nugget was disguised and pushed out in a wheelchair to confront the audience. People paid $5 a couple to guess who the bloke in the wheelchair was and no-one guessed it was Nugget.

When we talk about the function, Nugget's eyes light up. 'I thought someone would have guessed it was me. Anyway it was a great night. My sister, Di, came with me and she also enjoyed the night.'

Current Port Magpies coach Tim Ginever, who played in seven premierships—1988, 1989, 1990, 1992, 1994, 1995 and 1996—first met Nugget at a street corner in the middle of the city. Ginever recalls: 'It must have been in the early 80s. Nugget rushed up to me at the traffic lights and started enthusing about Port Magpies. I was a purchasing officer for Balfours at the time, so I was in town a fair bit and I was always running into Nugget. He wasn't just mad on the Port Magpies, he was a great influence about the club. He even came to barrack for the Crows before the Power began and that was due mainly to his knowing Tony McGuinness and Chris McDermott.'[44]

Given that Nugget has delivered special talks to the South Australian cricket team, the Australian Test cricket team,

Port Power and Goodwood Saints, you could easily assume that Nug must have also addressed the Maggies.

But Ginever says that's not the case. 'I know he gave the Power a pep-talk and that it was a raging success. We've had Nugget down to training and I love the way he's always so positive, but so far he's not given us one of his special rev-up speeches. We must have Nug talk to the group.'[45]

A while back Nugget and I ventured into the city from Kent Town, a considerable walk for us both. We stopped at a traffic light and Nug excitedly announced that he was flying to Sydney in a few days time.

'What's happening, Nug?'

'Oh, I can't say anything—it's a secret.'

'You can tell me, Nug.'

'No, I can't, it's a secret. Uncle Boof's coming over on the same plane with me and my sister Diane.'

I twigged. The recently retired Adam Gilchrist was now with Channel Nine. He was a certain target for Nine's old favourite, *This is Your Life*.

'Please—shoosh—don't tell anyone. I'll be in trouble. It is a secret,' Nug said with genuine concern.

'It's okay, mate,' I assured him. 'Your secret's safe.'

All those who know Nugget respect his integrity and ability to keep a confidence. As this incident reminded me, Nugget lives by his 'What goes on tour, stays on tour' philosophy.

A few yards on we bumped into Port Power champion Peter Burgoyne. He was having a coffee with his mates, former AFL players Troy and Shane Bond. The footballers greeted Nugget like a long-lost cousin. That this chance meeting occurred just three days after Port's 'capitulation' against Carlton—Port lost by 12 points after leading by 37 points at the start of the last quarter—says a lot about the players' genuine affection for Nugget.

He was, of course, his usual positive self. 'Don't worry fellas, you'll win next time and win well. You'll keep winning and make the final eight.'

Port's next match was against the all-powerful Geelong, the club that massacred them in the 2007 grand final. Few people held much hope that Port could beat the Cats at their home at Kardinia Park. Nugget was among that few.

'You will win on Sunday,' Nugget smiled, giving the double thumbs up to Peter Burgoyne.

Those words reflect Nugget's football life. Since he first set foot on Alberton Oval, more than 50 years ago, his support for the players has never wavered. From Port Adelaide to Port Power, from the Crows to the Goodwood Saints, Nugget's sincerity and positive attitude are recurring themes—and for this, they have all embraced him.

'You will win,' he tells them all, with a double thumbs up. 'You will win.'

Notes

1   Lawrie Jervis, *Sunday Mail*, October, 1954
2   Bob McLean, *Sunday Mail*, October, 1954
3   *The News*, Adelaide 1975, from the Barry Rees collection
4   Bob McLean, *The News*, 1955
5   John Cahill, *The News*, 1988
6   Josh Francou to author, July 2008
7   *From Port to a Power*, Bruce Abernethy, Wakefield Press, 1997, p.55
8   ibid.
9   Graham Cornes in the Port Magpies dressing-room immediately after his team lost the 1990 premiership.
10 Tony McGuiness to author, June 2008
11 ibid.
12 Kevin Sheedy, *The Australian*, 1997
13 Tony McGuiness to author, June 2008
14 Terry Blunden to author, February 2008
15 Hans Ellenbroek to author, May 2008
16 ibid.
17 Charlie Thomas to author, May 2008
18 David Bartel to author, May 2008
19 Kane Cornes to author, May 2008
20 Brett Ebert to author, May 2008
21 Stewart Cochrane to author, May 2008
22 Stuart Dew to author, July 2008
23 ibid.
24 ibid.
25 ibid.
26 Warren Tredrea to author, May 2008
27 Stephen Salopek to author, May 2008
28 Chad Cornes to author, May 2008
29 Jacob Surjen to author, June 2008
30 Brendon Lade to author, May 2008
31 Dean Brogan to author, May 2008
32 Michael Wilson to author, May 2008
33 Michael Pettigrew to author, May 2008
34 Mark Williams to author, May 2008
35 ibid.
36 ibid.
37 ibid.

38 ibid.
39 ibid.
40 Adam Kingsley to author, June 2008
41 Matthew Primus to author, June 2008
42 Matthew Richardson to author, May 2008
43 ibid.
44 Tim Ginever to author, June 2008
45 ibid.

CHAPTER 7

Nugget:
A shining light

Nugget has had little formal education, yet in ways he amazes and delights everyone who knows him with his insight and his perception.

Is Nugget a teacher?

Is Nugget a leader?

Perhaps we could not classify him as either a teacher or a leader in any academic definition; however, Nugget does teach us and he does lead by example.

For half a century Nugget has been unwittingly teaching a succession of club, State and Australian cricketers, and amateur and professional footballers, about the true meaning of life. Just as adults learn from children, we learn from Nugget, who has a child-like view of the world.

Nugget has learnt by experience: he watches and listens,

and absorbs knowledge. He adheres to the old Chinese proverb, 'I hear and I forget. I see and I remember. I do and I understand.'

In theory Barry Jarman and David Rowe could have gone with Nugget when he went out to get the lunches every day. Wisely, neither man did so; although Jarman, intrigued by Nugget's insistence that he accept money for only four lunch orders, once followed him to to see what he was doing. Jarman discovered that Nugget had worked things out; he had found, in his own inimitable fashion, how to solve a problem.

Perhaps it was on that day that Jarman realised the specialness of Nugget. He might have been slow in some things—as Wendy Page says, 'Aren't we all'—but he is very clever in other ways.[1]

David Rowe and Barry Jarman unknowingly adhered to E.M. Forster's adage, 'Spoon feeding in the long run teaches us nothing, but the shape of the spoon.' At Rowe & Jarman, Nugget was encouraged and guided, but he was left to work it out for himself. If he didn't understand something, he asked questions. Nugget persisted until he got the message loud and clear. As time progressed, Nugget gained confidence, often coming up with one-liners that astounded workmates, as well as his cricket and football heroes.

Henry Adams said, 'A teacher affects eternity: he can never tell where his influence stops.' Nugget may be totally unaware of his influence, but he has taught us and continues to teach us about the simple courtesies and goodness of life. He possesses the most respectable manners and his particular 'no-strings-attached' brand of giving is etched onto his soul.

One of Nugget's many long-time friends is Sally Schultz. Now a speech pathologist, Sally was 15 when she began working at Rowe & Jarman. Sally says: 'Nugget was wonderful. His manners and his memory are incredible. He maintains that he got my husband Steve and I together, and while we were courting Nugget was always encouraging us. We'd be in Steve's car and Nugget would knock on the window, his smiling face would appear, he'd give the thumbs-up sign and say time and again, "Hubba-hubba".'[2]

Just like 'much, much' in Nugget-speak means a little more than good, 'hubba-hubba' was an encouragment. Nugget could already hear wedding bells.

'I got Sally and Steve together,' Nugget says. 'They were both at the shop, Sally in the office and Steve was a buyer.'

'So you are something of a cupid, Nugget?'

'Oh, no, Rowdy. I don't know Cupie or whatever you said, but I do know I brought Sally and Steve together—and they are still together.'

Then he adds: ' I don't know what it is—but I've got it!'

He's got 'it' alright. Everyone loves being in his company. Nugget brings the best out of people. During research into this book, I've looked at hundreds of photographs of Nugget with an extraordinary array of people. Whether they're the

Prime Minister, the captain of the Australian cricket team, the captain of Port Power, or the lady across the road from where he lives, the person in the photo is always happy.

Always.

Sally recalls Nugget always giving her, along with all staff members at Rowe & Jarman, a 'specially wrapped Christmas present'.

Sally got to know Nugget and his giving ways; however, it was only when she began helping youngsters with speech difficulties that she realised how much she had really learnt from Nugget. Sally says: 'It's only since I have been away from Rowe & Jarman that I have come to fully realise the amazing impact Nugget has had on my professional life.

'The incredible giving by Barry Jarman and David Rowe in the workplace has helped create an environment for Nugget to blossom. He has improved remarkably—in all ways—since I first met him in 1977.

'The experts tell us that the human brain does not allow us to grow intellectually after the age of 30. Well, I have seen quite amazing improvement in Nugget from that age right up until today. Over the past 30 years Nugget has come on a treat. He is quick with his repartee and comes up with terrific one-liners.

'Having watched Nugget at work, and seeing him grow in confidence, has given me the vision to pass on hope and belief in my patients. Thanks to Nugget and his development, I realise that you simply do not "keep the lid" on anyone. Given the right circumstances everyone can improve and grow.

'There's no doubt the love and support of his sister Diane and their family, plus that caring working environment at Rowe & Jarman, have given Nugget what I call "the magic mix".

'I look at the kids I work with through different eyes these days. Nugget has given me the confidence to give these youngsters belief and hope in a bright future. Thanks to the experience I have had observing and knowing Nugget, I never close the lid on anyone.'[3]

Steve Schultz met Nugget's dad, Ray Rees, at Rowe & Jarman. Steve says: 'I didn't know Ray from a bar of soap. BJ [Jarman] introduced us. Ray told me to listen to what Nugget is saying. "You will only get an idea of what he is going to do from what he says. If he writes something you won't understand it."

'Nugget's writing was like some ancient hieroglyphic which he alone could decipher. But things changed. He got better with words and expression, and the improvement was remarkable, a beautiful thing to see.'[4]

These days Nugget writes often, especially for the countless kids wanting his autograph at the cricket or the football. He even has collectors of memorabilia write to him, asking for his autograph. And Nugget's autograph ends up in the same collector's folder as Ricky Ponting, Michael Clarke and Brett Lee.

As a buyer, Steve Schultz used to meet a variety of sports agents and salesmen. Steve recalls: 'Some people didn't know what to make of Nugget. He'd shake their hands and with those he knew well he'd pat them on the back. These people soon got to know that Nugget was part of the Rowe & Jarman family.'[5]

As with the cricketers and the footballers, part of the rite of passage to success and being part of the scene at Rowe & Jarman was to embrace the specialness that is Nugget Rees. Steve says, 'At the shop he was loved by all. He even went out to parties where there were only teenagers, kids about 17 or 18. His influence crossed all age groups.'[6]

One day a fellow turned up to Steve's office. While he cannot recall the businessman's name, Steve says he was a 'high flyer with Santos', a large Adelaide company which specialised in oil exploration. 'Nugget was asked to get a few bats signed during the Adelaide Test. He returned with three full-sized bats signed by every member of the Australian Test team. When I gave the bats back to the man from Santos, he looked at one of the bats and the names and inquired about a signature at the bottom of the bat. "Who's that?" he asked.

'I explained that what he was looking at was the autograph of Nugget Rees, a member of every Australian cricket team which plays a Test on the Adelaide Oval since the year dot.'[7]

Nugget had become the face of Rowe & Jarman sports store.

One day a small man in a grey suit arrived in the store. He wore a felt hat and carried a 'lived-in' brown leather briefcase. After signing a number of cricket bats, Sir Donald Bradman placed his brown leather briefcase to one side and shook Steve Schultz's hand. 'Sir Donald said, "Thanks Steve. I'm off now. You know Nugget walks down the street and everyone in Adelaide knows him. I walk down Rundle Mall and no-one has a clue who I am." I'm sure Sir Donald was glad that he wasn't recognised, given all the hype and publicity and attention he'd experienced over his long life, but it was an interesting observation.'[8]

Two of Nugget's best mates are former AFL champion footballers Tony McGuinness and Chris McDermott. Both worked in a selling capacity at Rowe & Jarman and both captained the Adelaide Crows football team. They also won All-Australian selection.

On May 30, 1996, the McGuinness-McDermott Foundation was launched. The idea for the Foundation came to the footballers in 1991 when they were playing for the Crows and the club first entered the AFL. They were greatly influenced by two seriously ill boys, Crows fans, they met. Chris McDermott met Nathan MacLean in 1991. They developed a strong friendship, although Nathan's life expectancy was limited. He had a brain tumour. Nathan was Chris' biggest fan, but sadly he died in February 1993. Tony McGuinness met Nicholas Berry in 1992 and the pair hit it off immediately. Tony followed Nicholas' fight against the odds: he had kidney cancer and he died of the disease in December 1994.

The courage of those two boys touched the hearts of the champion footballers and they were determined to see what they could do to help medical science win the battle against a variety of diseases. Tony McGuinness says, 'The charter has been to raise awareness and funds for all areas of oncology treatment for these special children and their families in South Australia.'[9]

In the twelve years since it began, the McGuinness-McDermott Foundation, established in the memory of Nathan MacLean and Nicholas Berry, has raised more than $9 million for the Womens and Childrens Hospital in Adelaide. It has completed 13 major projects, including the Ronald McDonald Clinic worth more than $250,000; a dialysis unit to support seriously ill children in the children's renal clinic; an adolescent ward; an X-ray machine; central water system; paediatric theatres holding bay redevelopment; an endocrine unit; and an MRI (Magnetic Resonance Imaging) machine.

Both men are a credit to South Australia. Their work in raising money for sick children simply cannot be measured in dollar terms.

Over the duration of the Foundation's life-time, Nugget has worked alongside Tony and Chris, visiting seriously ill children in hospital. 'Nug does an important job, meeting people, running messages and performing all manner of important jobs at our major fundraiser, the Slowdown,' Chris McDermott says.[10]

The Slowdown is a football match played between retired Port Power and Adelaide Crows players. Occasionally, a celebrity player is invited from other sports (tennis star and Crows fan Lleyton Hewitt among them). And Nugget is always there to help.

Chris McDermott has gotten to know Nugget very well over the years and when Chris bought the Sturt Arcade Hotel in Grenfell Street, which was a watering hole for Rowe & Jarman staff for many a long year, and turned it into the Players' Bar, Nugget often helped out there.

'Nug would deliver plates and, of course, meet and greet everyone,' Chris says. 'I have found Nug to be super loyal, with great energy and enthusiasm. That's what we all love about him.

'Kevin Sheedy set some sort of record—27 years coaching Essendon—but Nugget has been playing and coaching cricket and football for nearly 50 years. He's a mile ahead of Sheeds.'[11]

Tony McGuinness is, of course, also the man behind the Barry 'Nugget' Rees Trust, which helps Nugget, his sister Diane and brother-in-law Rusty maintain Nugget's lifestyle. He says: 'Leaving the shop left a big void in Nugget's life. He was there for such a long time and each day was an adventure. Then it ended.

'I thought Nugget and his family needed a little extra

assistance. His sister, Diane, has done a wonderful job in looking after him. Nugget is incredibly reliant on Di and we just wanted to take a bit of pressure off there.

'"A Night with Nugget" was used to kick-start funds for a trust to be set up for him—the Barry 'Nugget' Rees Trust Fund. The Trust Fund helps lessen the financial burden on Nugget's sister Diane and her husband Rusty Smith. It helps with his travel, clothing and medical expenses. From time to time Nugget might need a set of new clothes; such was the case when he went to Sydney for Adam Gilchrist's *This is Your Life* television special.'

'We didn't want to see Nugget sitting at home all day in his retirement. He needs access to a vehicle to pick him up and take him to football training, or the cricket, or a function. And it is not just a matter of getting a vehicle. It has got to be with someone he trusts.'[12]

So if Tony McGuinness or Darren Lehmann cannot take Nugget to a certain venue, such as Alberton Oval or AAMI Stadium, Nugget phones up an Adelaide chauffeur service.

McGuinness says: 'He knows all the drivers by his very enquiring and loving nature. Nugget would no doubt know all the drivers on a first name basis and would know their wives and partners and their children.

'The big thing here is trust. Nugget trusts the drivers and occasionally I meet these drivers and they think it's remarkable the people Nugget meets at the other end of the journey.'[13]

Nugget would be dropped off at Adelaide Oval and as he got out of the car Ricky Ponting or Michael Clarke would say, 'Good morning Nugget', and the driver would stand there in amazement.

The Trust Fund, McGuinness says, is very much about making sure Nugget is comfortable. 'When Nugget was working at the shop in the city he had easy access to everybody. He's now removed from that environment, notwithstanding he does work one day a week at Sam Parkinson Marketing, but we want him out there regularly.

'He responds best when he is familiar with the people around him. He is very wary of people he is not familiar with and familiarity is crucial to his well-being.

'When Nugget is dealing with the people he trusts, then he's comfortable. So we try and surround him with the people he trusts.

'Money can't buy the value of his lifestyle. Lots of good things have happened for him.'[14]

But while the Fund has been given financial boosts with the occasional fundraising dinner on Nugget's behalf—the most famous of all being 'A Night with Nugget' which drew more than 500 people and a cast of international sports stars, especially Test cricketers—time has gone by and the Fund is diminishing quickly.

McGuinness has now produced a concept paper on establishing a Barry 'Nugget' Rees Foundation. The vision is to celebrate the unique life of Nugget. It's mission is to provide access to sporting experiences for people with integration difficulties. And it's objective is to raise funds through events or auctions of unique sporting memorabilia from sporting identities who have had an association with Nugget. McGuinness wants to involve big business, the SACA, leading sports and business identities, the media, and the South Australian Sport and Recreation Association for People with Integration Difficulties Inc (SASRAPID). Through the work of the McGuinness-McDermott Foundation and the Barry 'Nugget' Rees Foundation and Trust Fund, sportsmen like McGuinness and McDermott are showing that it is possible to give back to those who inspire them—whether it's Nathan MacLean, Nicholas Berry or Barry 'Nugget' Rees.

Nugget's bedroom is a sporting memorabilia collector's dream. There are hats and bats and balls and books.

With my interest in books, I was drawn to Nugget's packed bookcase. There are hundreds of sporting books crammed into his bookshelves—cricket, football, more cricket. Most of the books have been given to Nugget by the sport stars themselves. What do they have to say about our 'Man of the Century'?

In *Roy, Going for Broke,* by Andrew Symonds with Steven Gray (Hardie Grant Books, Melbourne, 2007), Symonds wrote: 'To Nugget, The heart and soul of the Adelaide dressing-room.'

In *Hookesy*, by David Hookes with Alan Shiell (ABC, Australia, 1993), Hookes wrote: 'To Nugget, Thanks for your friendship and help over my career. Your presence was always an inspiration. Best wishes, Hookesy.'

In *By Hook or By Cut* (Investigator Press, Adelaide, 1970), Les Favell wrote: 'My old mate, best wishes, Les Favell.'

From Mark Waugh, in *Mark Waugh, The Biography* (HarperSports, Sydney, 2002): 'To Nugget, Thank you for your friendship and support over the years.'

In *Shane Warne, My Autobiography* (Hodder & Stoughton, London, 2001), by Shane Warne with Richard Hobson, Warne delivers a lengthy message: 'To Nugget, Thank you for your support, mate. You are a star. You are an inspiration to us all and your support to all Australian cricket teams over the years has been very much appreciated. You are always welcome in the dressing-room. It's great to have you around. Your friend always, Warnie!'

In another book on Warne, an unauthorised biography put together by Ken Piesse, part of Warne's message to Nugget is written in capital letters on the title page: 'NOT MY BOOK, NUG!!'

In *Walking and Victory* (MacMillan, Melbourne, 2003), Adam Gilchrist's note to his friend reads: 'Nugget, Thanks for your friendship and support. You're a true gentleman.'

Fast-bowler Jason Gillespie, who has had a good deal to do with Nugget over the course of his career with South

Australia and Australia, in *Dizzy, the Jason Gillespie Story*, by Jason Gillespie with Laurie Colliver (Harper Collins, Melbourne, 2007), writes: 'To my great mate, "Nug, Nug", Thank you so much for all your support over the years buddy. Having you around makes the game so much more enjoyable. You are a true "legend" mate. Love ya big guy, Dizzy.'

Darren Lehmann, in his book, *Worth the Wait* (Hardie Grant Books, Melbourne, 2004), writes this tribute: 'To Nugget, You are a champion and I love having you around. You are a great friend and a loyal supporter. And one of my best mates. Look after yourself champ. Many more hundreds from you to come. Best wishes, your mate, Darren Lehmann.'

In 1997, Ian Healy signed his book *The Ian Healy Story* (Swan Publishing, Perth, 1997): 'To Nugget, You're a champion and an inspiration.'

Former Australian captain Steve Waugh, in *Images of Waugh, A cricketer's journey* (HarperSports, Sydney, 1998), wrote: 'To Nugget, You're the star of the book, with best wishes always, Steve Waugh.'

In *T.J. Over the Top* (Information Australia, Melbourne, 1999), by Terry Jenner with Ken Piesse, Jenner wrote: 'To my old mate Nugget. You are an inspiration to us all. Your friendship is special.'

There are many, many more cricket books in Nugget's collection—including one signed by the 'Little Master',

Indian batsman Sachin Tendulkar—but one of the earliest is *My Country's Keeper* (Pelham Books, London, 1965) by Wally Grout, talking to Frank Callaghan. Grout was the Test wicket-keeper in the Richie Benaud and Alan Davidson eras. He played at Adelaide Oval in the early to mid-1960s, where he got to know Nugget. Grout wrote, 'To Barry, Best wishes, Wally Grout.' Nugget collected that autograph so far back that Grout was calling him 'Barry'.

Nugget hasn't as many books signed by his football heroes; however, he does have books from Kevin Sheedy, Gavin Wanganeen and Andrew Jarman, who calls Nug, 'my best mate'. In his copy of *The Night Marcus Won the Flag* (Wakefield Press, Adelaide, 2004), by Jenny and Mark Williams, Williams has written: 'To Nugget, turn on your power'.

But perhaps the most treasured book of all was one given to Nugget in 1979 by his father, Ray Rees. The book, *The Home for Incurables, the first 100 years*, by Colin Kerr (Lutheran Publishing House, Adelaide, 1979) is treasured by Nugget because he received it from his hero, his dad. Ray Rees was secretary of the Home for Incurables (later to be re-named the Julia Farr Centre) for many years.

If there has been one constant throughout his life that has allowed Nugget to shine, it is his family. His parents, whom he still misses daily, and his sisters, Diane and Pam, have nurtured Nugget into the person he is today.

Tony McGuinness says that Nugget and Diane have a 'beautiful relationship'. 'Di's contribution to Nugget in terms of a sister-to-brother commitment is nothing like I have ever seen or am likely to see,' McGuinness says. 'Nugget trusts Di totally. Given where Nugget is at in his life, that devotion and trust he places in her is beautiful to see.'[15]

In their early childhood it was big brother Barry who looked after Pam and Diane from the time when they were toddlers, with a lovely brotherly protectiveness. Now, it is Diane and Pam who look after their brother. They recognise his special spirit and are protective of it.

When Ray Rees was terminally ill with cancer, one of his biggest concerns was Nugget's future welfare. Di explains: 'As Dad's health deteriorated, Nug came to live with us at Cheltenham Street, Malvern. It was out first home. Rusty and I purchased the house a couple of months before we married in 1972. Dad helped us buy it. Nugget was happy moving in with us. He thought he was helping, looking after the children. At the time Corey was about 12 and Cassie, 10. He was lovely and he was a great help around the house and fitted in well. But I don't think Nug realised how ill our dad was; Nug thought he'd come to live with us for a little while and go back home.

'Nugget was with us for six months while Dad was very ill, having treatment. Then, when we knew he wasn't going to get any better, Nugget went back home to be with Dad. When it did come to the crunch, near the end of Dad's life,

Nug again came to stay. It was Dad's wish. He knew that Nug wasn't going to stay where he was, with Thea. So he probably wanted to put something in place to make sure that Nugget would be alright, because Dad nurtured Nug all his life and looked after him.

'Right at the end, Dad knew how well Nugget fitted into our family and that was one way he could "let go", because he was confident that Nug would be okay.

'Pam had Barry occasionally, maybe a night or two, but never long-term. It was never decided that Nugget would come and stay with us when Dad passed away, until Dad passed away. Then, Pam and I sat down with Rusty and Neil to discuss Nug's future and what was the best thing for him. Having had Nug with us, I guess it was just accepted that he was coming to live with us.

'So Nugget moved in with us permanently and he was fine about it. When Dad passed away he seemed to get over it better than a lot of us. That's what they do, people like Nug; they get very upset, but then they turn the other shoulder and get on with life, they move on a lot quicker than either you or I probably can.

'Rusty and I never really talked about Nugget moving in. I guess Rusty knew when he married me that Nugget was part of our life and that something might happen one day and Nugget would be with us.

'So Nug coming to live with us was a natural progression. He was part of our family.

'At the time I was very upset about losing Dad. I think having Nugget staying with us helped me get through the grieving process. I had to deal with having someone else in the family and make sure things were alright with my children, with Rusty and with Nug. So it probably kept me busy.'[16]

Sadly, when Ray Rees died, the house on Grove Street, along with the furniture, even precious, irreplaceable family photographs, were all left to his second wife, Thea. Diane says, 'Dad was good enough to set up other bits and pieces for Pam and me, which Pam sorted out with Dad. He felt Nugget would be comfortable living with one of us and that he'd be okay. So the way Dad had things set up, nothing was in Nug's name. It was in either Pam's or my name.

'Thea wanted out of the house. She had been searching for a new house before Dad passed away. When Thea found a house, she wanted to settle on Grove Street straightaway. We had to sell our house in Cheltenham Street, Malvern, within six weeks to be able to move in to the family home at Grove Street.

'Thea kept everything, all the family silver, the old radiogram, all the furniture that Mum and Dad had collected over the years. Things she kept had far more sentimental value to us than to her.'[17]

It was a tough time for Diane and Rusty. They had two young children and now Nugget. Then Rusty, as master plumber, fell off a roof and badly injured his back, knees and wrist. He was unable to work full-time for three years. Diane was working where she still works today and kept the family going until Rusty recovered from his injuries. To their dismay they had to sell the family home at Grove Street and move into a smaller place in Colonel Light Gardens, where they have lived since 1991.

Change for Nugget can be a huge disruption for him. Diane explains: 'If you say you are going to be somewhere and you're not, he gets cross. So when we moved we were thinking of the future, of his security and peace of mind. We put him foremost in our thoughts and because he had been with us, we felt he'd be fine.

'Nugget came to our family thinking that his main aim was helping me with Corey and Cassie. They were young so they've had Nug in their lives for a long time. Cassie turned 30 the other week and it's lovely to see now the roles have reversed. Rusty and I go away for a night or two and Corey or Cassie comes in to see that Nug's alright. They look after Nug now.'[18]

Diane and Rusty's son, Corey, has followed his father into the plumbing game. Corey believes his Uncle Nugget's influence on many aspects of his life was huge: 'One day it really hit me. I picked up the phone and the voice on the other end said, "Oh, this is Steve Waugh, I'd like to speak with Nugget... Sorry to have missed him. Can you please ask Nug to ring me back when he can?"

'I was amazed. Later I saw how Uncle Nug would mix with all the sports stars. His mixing with the Test cricketers really inspired me to represent Australia in sport.'[19]

Corey plays ice hockey, a huge sport in North America and in Europe but relatively small in Australia. 'Thanks to Uncle Nugget's inspiration I went on to play for Australia at junior level. I got to see the the US, Canada, Europe. When Uncle Nug went to England in 1989 that was a further inspiring time for me and I wanted to travel to faraway places.'[20]

Nugget used to go and watch Rusty play ice hockey at the Thebarton Ice Rink. Later he saw Corey develop in the sport. 'Yes, I liked the ice hockey,' Nugget says, 'but it was too cold over there. I liked it when the restaurant was there, then that was gone. I was left with the cold.'

Corey recalls going to his Aunty Pam's place at Victor Harbor every summer: 'The kids would play cricket and always Uncle Nug wanted to umpire. He never wanted to play, only umpire. Cricket and football were Uncle Nug's go and I can tell you that you stayed clear of him if Port Adelaide lost. With Uncle Nug there are extremes: he's either very happy or he's very upset. There's no middle or grey area. Uncle Nug takes everything to heart. Usually he's very upset when the Power lose or the cricket team is struggling.'[21]

Corey says that apart from inspiring him to work hard to get where he wanted to be in his chosen sport, 'Uncle Nug has taught me a great deal about how people should be treated. He's taught me about respect for elders, about good manners. As you know he has the most impeccable manners.'[22]

Just as Nugget used help look after Corey and Cassie, he now has a role in the lives of Corey and his wife Sarah's two childen, Kalyre, 8, and Connor, 5. Corey says: 'One day each week Uncle Nug picks up my two children from primary school. He takes the kids over to a park near the school and lets them play for a long time. Kalyre and Conner eagerly look forward to it.

'I think a relative of the Test umpire, Daryl Harper, teaches at the school, so Uncle Nugget often bumps into Daryl and it takes a long time for him to get home.

'Uncle Nug is a great influence on me and my family. It is my wish that my kids develop with the same impeccable manners as their Uncle Nug. In fact, if they grow up with half the manners he has, I'll be very happy. He's a beautiful person.'[23]

Diane's daughter Cassie was only ten years of age when Nugget came to live with their family on a full-time basis. 'It was pretty natural,' Cassie says. 'I think I liked the novelty of having another person in the house. Uncle Nug is such a lovely man, a huge part of our family. But I didn't really understand the impact he had with other people until the party we held to mark his 50th birthday. All these people from different walks of life, and celebrity sports people, they embraced Uncle Nug with utter respect and love—it really brought home to me how others regarded him as a very special human being.'[24]

At the time of writing, Cassie and her partner Billy are two months away from having their first child. 'Uncle Nug comes up to me and rubs my tummy and always says, "Cassie, it's going to be a boy, I reckon. Yep, it will be a boy."'[25]

No doubt Nugget is thinking ahead. A boy means another cricketer in the family, or a footballer, or both.

Cassie, like her brother, observes that 'Uncle Nug has his ups and down emotionally'. 'We see that on the home-front,' she says, 'but it is no different from any of us. But for Uncle Nug, it's the cricket and the football—and whether his team wins—which are the major factors in any change of mood.'[26]

Ray Rees would be justly proud of the way in which Diane and Rusty have cared for Nugget, just as Ray would be amazed at the change in Nugget and what he has achieved. Diane has a simple philosophy: 'You adapt and cope with what life throws at you. Whatever the challenge, you adapt. You have to work at things. Take marriage, you have to work at marriage.'[27]

In this aspect, Diane says her husband Rusty 'has been marvellous'. 'People often say to me how wonderful he was to accept Nugget into our home. Rusty and Nugget have grown together. When I first met Rusty he was so shy, he's laidback and quiet even now, but the pair of them chat about the cricket or the football, even ice hockey. I never thought I'd see the day but Nug occasionally does sit alongside Rusty and watch the ice hockey.

'I know if something happened while I was away, Rusty and Nug would look after one another. It is a good feeling for me to know that—it's a comfort.'[28]

It hasn't always been easy for Di. These days, Nugget defers to her for everything. Wherever Nugget goes, be it to the football, or the cricket, lunch with Jason Gillespie, speaking at Rotary with David Rowe, or working at a McGuinness-McDermott Foundation, Diane knows where he is and who is with him.

'It hasn't always been that way,' Di admits. 'I had to work very hard to get to this stage. There were times when I didn't know where he was and I'd get cross. Just like when you are dealing with a child, we had to know where he was and what he was doing.

'I had to get some ground rules laid down. I said to Nug, "It's not fair, you've got to work in with the family." At first he didn't like that, he'd say a few words and go off in a huff to his room—he still does get in a huff and goes to his room if I don't let him do something.

'But if things ever do get a bit tense—and sometimes they do for Barry can get very strong-willed—I often refer him to Dad and say, "What would your father say?"

'We see a different side to Nugget. Other people don't see the side of how demanding he can be when he's at home. But he's lovely and he knows when I need time out. He knows to go to his room. Nug's pretty self-sufficient in that he has his own room, his television, his DVDs, his books, everything there that he needs. I would never tell him to go to his room, he knows when to go.

'There are little disagreements in all families which everyone has, but Nugget can't handle that. He gets very upset and very defensive. In Dad's second marriage, there was a lot of arguing between Dad and Thea—a lot—and Barry didn't like that at all.'[29]

Nugget has lots of extraordinary highs—days at Test cricket matches, lunch with Peter McIntyre or Darren Lehmann, days at the football, mixing with the best sporting stars around—and there inevitably has to be a let-down. After a day out on Cloud Nine, Nug can come to earth with a bit of thud. Diane makes the landing as soft as possible. 'With Nug there's some gift there, his caring nature and how people warm to him. People with a very busy lifestyle feel at ease and get pleasure over Nug being in their company. But they don't see the down side to Nug which we see.

'He will have been out having a lovely time and he will come home and I'll say, "I'll pack this away" and he will say "Oh, Diane stop fussing" and he will get cross with me. So he's got to calm down and I just pacify him. I just do what I have to do about the house and it's okay. Nug has to have something to look forward to otherwise he's not happy.

'When Nug is not happy about something, he comes to me. It might be about something written in the newspaper or he wants clarification about an issue; he relies on me to give him a full explanation.'[30]

Nugget won't get on a bus by himself, and Diane has promised their father that she wouldn't allow Nug to travel alone on a bus. Diane explains: 'A long time ago Barry was greatly upset by something which happened on a bus. I don't know the circumstances. It might have been someone making fun of him, but Dad said to me "Don't you ever let him get on a bus alone again".

'These days Nugget often rides a bus, but not alone. He often travels with Hans Ellenbroek, who doesn't drive, and it is usually a Thursday afternoon in winter when they catch a bus to attend training with the Goodwood Saints Football Club.

'One night Nug got back from training and he spoke enthusiastically about the bus trip. "Hans and I caught the 121 and we met..." Dad would be so proud of what Nug has achieved; he would not believe it's the same person.

'I guess being younger, Rusty and I have let Nug do a lot more things, much more than my father ever would have allowed. Dad was really both our mum and our dad. He set the rules and you either obeyed the rules or else. If Nug didn't have these wonderful opportunities, one wonders where he might be, but Nug makes his own friends.'[31]

While Ray Rees may have been overprotective of Nugget,

it was he who allowed Nugget to grow, in finding his son a job at Rowe & Jarman.

What might have become of Nugget had Ray not taken that step? Diane says, 'I don't know. I've often thought of that, but I reckon Dad would have found something for Nug. He was interested in a lot of things, like the cricket and the football and the trots, things Dad also liked. Nug loved everything Dad did. He looked up to Dad as his idol, his hero.'[32]

It is now 20 years since Ray Rees died.

'I still think about my dad, you know, Rowdy,' Nugget tells me in a whisper, his eyes welling. 'I do. I think of him a lot. He would be proud of me. I know he would be proud of me.'

Nugget's room fronts the street and he knows what is happening not only near the family home, but also along both sides of the street. For as far as the eye can see, Nugget observes the comings and goings. He'll know what time you go out and what time you return, who has visitors, who doesn't, when the rubbish truck comes.

'No-one slips past Nugget's front window without him spotting them,' Diane says. 'He is very good at watching what goes on. He got to know the postman and now the postman by-passes the letterbox and brings anything for Nugget right to the front door. When the postie comes, Nugget will whip out to see him. They have a great rapport. Nugget was invited to the postman's 40th birthday party.'[33]

At the time of writing, Nug's older sister, Pam, was receiving treatment for lymphatic cancer. She had been in remission for nearly two years before the discovery of a new outbreak. All the family are staying positive. 'Pam will be okay,' Nug says.

Diane's protective instinct comes to the fore: She didn't take Nugget to see Pam in the early aftermath of radiotherapy, because 'I don't want him to see her like that—it's not fair to Pam and it's not fair to Nug.'[34]

However, Diane adds that, 'Nug has come a long way in this area. You couldn't say the word "cancer" after Dad died. I think it's being out in the world. Now he can accept it. He's matured a good deal in that way.'[35]

Pam's children Hamish, Rebecca and Cameron, like Diane's children, all adore their Uncle Nugget. Nugget was a groomsman at Pam and Neil's wedding and is godfather to their first child, Hamish. Hamish, now a geologist, says, 'Nugget is genuine, loyal and he really loves all his relatives. He's very special.'[36]

Hamish remembers when Nugget used to take him to the South Australian dressing-room at Adelaide Oval to meet the players. 'That was amazing,' he says. He also recalls 'being dragged along to the greyhound racing and when Uncle Nugget was the official "catcher". He was also terrific as the umpire when the kids played cricket on holiday at Encounter Bay. All the lbw appeals were greeted with a very firm "not out"!'[37]

Rebecca Freeman recalls the adventures at Encounter Bay in summer and tells how her uncle taught her to float: 'Uncle Nug was always out in the ocean, floating on his back. We always knew it was him because his tummy was popping up in the air. He was a brilliant floater and he taught me to float, just as he taught us to make sand castles, and he always gave Cassie and me one more chance to bat when we played cricket in the backyard.

'Uncle Nug also got me a job at Chris McDermott's Players' Bar. It was then that I got to know Uncle Nug's "other life"; he'd be always mixing with the top cricketers and footballers. Uncle Nug used to help me with my footy tips. He was Crows then, dare I say it. That was for a year or two before Port got into the AFL.

'One Christmas lunch when all the family were there, Uncle Nug started jumping about in his seat yelling, "There's a fish under the table, a fish flapping!" Our dog, a whippet, had grabbed a shank of lamb and was shaking her head, the bone smacking Uncle Nug's leg. Now when Uncle Nug's at dinner with us we say, "Watch out for the fish under the table." Uncle Nugget has got a heart of gold.'[38]

Cameron completed a PhD in Philosophy at Flinders University. He gives talks here and overseas about the parables of Jesus Christ and challenges some of the accepted views of the biblical Jesus story. Cameron says: 'I deliver lots of speeches and I always go to Nugget for advice. Uncle Nug told me: "Don't be nervous, Cameron. Speak up and out to the audience and give your speech from the heart. You'll be fine."

'Nugget's life and his amazing development over the years really does show us that quality can show up in the most unexpected places. I know that I am a far better person by knowing Nugget. He shares great joy and he tells us all about what really matters in this life.'[39]

A few years back Cameron stayed with Nugget for two weeks while Diane and Rusty were away interstate on holiday. Spending that time together, Cameron and Nugget got to know each other better. Cameron recalls: 'We went on long walks together, shared the spa and had a few beers at night. We just talked about things in general, about life. What I noticed about all of this was that I was supposed to be looking after him, yet Nugget really was looking after me. I realised then that he was a lot more independent and capable that many people thought. It was a special time.'[40]

The hardships faced by Nugget's family—his mother's long illness, then his father dying after a lengthy battle with cancer—have helped shape his character. Nugget is respectful to everyone but he has long been loving and caring to the vulnerable in our society, the frail, the aged and the very young.

For 42 years Sue Bennie has been a regular at Adelaide Oval Test matches. Sue loves cricket with a passion and it's something now shared by her three children, Jessie, 17,

Mitchell, 15 and Courtney, 8. Over the years Sue had collected lots of caps signed by the Test men. And as her children grew so too did her collection of memorabilia. She had signed photographs, bats, balls and caps. They all became a special part of the family group.

Tragically, in January 2008, the Bennies' house burnt to the ground. The family lost all their possessions, every skerrick of cricket memorabilia, their furniture, everything. And they had no insurance on the house and contents. It was a shattering experience for Sue and her family.

Nugget has known Sue Bennie for years. He would say hello to Sue, as he does to everyone he knows at Adelaide Oval during match day, on the lengthy walk from the Phil Riding Gates at the southern end to the players' dressing-room in the Members' Stand. Upset about Sue Bennie's plight, Nugget decided to do something about it. He rang his mate, Gavin Lincoln, who he used to work with at Rowe & Jarman and who now runs a sports clothing outlet, Jaxsport, in Kilburn.

'Nugget ringing me wasn't unusual,' Lincoln laughed. 'He rings me every day of the year, and I mean seven days a week, every week of every year. Nug told me about Sue Bennie's tough luck and he said that he wanted to organise something.'[41]

Jaxsport supplies cricket clothing to Adelaide clubs and the SANFL football gear. Nugget told Lincoln that he would get hold of an Australian one-day international shirt, have it signed by all of the Australian one-day team and then have Gavin Lincoln organise for the shirt to be framed so he could present it to Sue Bennie.

Sue remembers the day Nugget gave her the framed shirt with all the Australian players' signatures on it: 'Nugget was in his cricket gear, he was even wearing batting gloves and he gave me a big hug. I said, "Now don't you make me cry, Nugget", but I had tears rolling down my cheeks.

'The children and I were blown away by Nugget's gift. One of the things destroyed in the fire was a match ball signed by Brian Lara [the great West Indian batsman]. That was, of course, along with many other things, irreplaceable. But Nugget's giving has helped ease the pain of all our losses.

'Nugget is such a caring, loving person. He's an angel.'[42]

When they first started to accompany their mother to the cricket, the Bennie children didn't know a lot about the legend of Nugget Rees. Sue recalls: 'One day we were standing there and Nugget offered to sign my son's hat. He signed and when Nugget left, my son, Mitchell, then aged 11, said, "Who's Nugget?"

'Now when we go to the cricket, Mitchell says, "Hey Mum, where's Nugget? I hope we get to see him today."'[43]

Two-thirds of the way through the football season last year, with Nugget's beloved Port Power sitting down the ladder with 4 wins and 11 losses, he rang Sue as she was driving to Flinders Park Hospital, where she works as a receptionist. 'He said, "Good morning Sue, how are you? It's

Nugget Rees here. Are you okay? How are you? Hope you are alright? The Power can still do it. We only have to win our last eight games in a row. We can do it." Nugget is just such a positive person. He's such a joy.'[44]

Soon after Adam Gilchrist had hung up his boots for the last time, Nugget had Gilly sign the pair of pads he wore in his last match and Nugget presented the signed pads to Sue Bennie and her children.

Soon after, Nugget flew to Sydney with sister Di and Uncle Boof for a guest appearance in Adam Gilchrist's *This Is Your Life* program on Channel Nine, Nugget was admitted to hospital to have a pacemaker fitted. Nugget's heart-rate had dropped alarmingly to the high 30s (a rate of 60 is considered the minimum) and the operation was essential for his wellbeing. On the Saturday, Nugget went to Melbourne to watch his beloved Port Power, then on the Monday he was in a hospital bed. A day after his operation Nugget welcomed a stream of well-wishers. One visitor really made Nugget's hospital stay. In walked Adam Gilchrist.

'Now, how are you Nugget?'

'I'm fine Gilly. I've just had a peace-maker put in.'[45]

It could be Steve Waugh, Adam Gilchrist, Ricky Ponting, Michael Clarke, Shaun Burgoyne, Chad Cornes or Josh Francou walking down a city street, and the instant they spot Nugget, they are drawn to him.

Nugget is a shining light. He enriches our lives in an extraordinary way. While he isn't religious in the strict sense of the word—only going to church when 'I go to weddings'—there is something on the cusp of the divine about him, possibly because the sprit within him reaches out to us all.

The Very Reverend Dr John Shepherd, Anglican Dean of Perth, summed it up when he said: 'It's like Nugget is already in heaven. He exudes joy and love and those lucky enough to meet him are being given an idea of what we can expect in the after-life: Here he stands; the happy, smiling messenger angel giving us a foretaste of what lies in store.[46]

To meet Nugget is to be immediately warmed by his spirit.

To know him is to love him.

Notes

1   Wendy Page to author, Sydney, February 2008
2   Sally Schultz to author, June 2008
3   ibid.
4   Steve Schultz to author, June 2008
5   ibid.
6   ibid.
7   ibid.
8   ibid.
9   Tony McGuinness to author, June 2008
10 Chris McDermott to author, July 2008
11 ibid.
12 Tony McGuinness to author, July 2008
13 ibid.
14 ibid.
15 ibid.
16 Diane Smith to author, July 2008
17 ibid.
18 ibid.
19 Corey Smith to author, July 2008
20 ibid.
21 ibid.
22 ibid.
23 ibid.
24 Cassie Smith to author, July 2008
25 ibid.
26 ibid.
27 Diane Smith to author, July 2008
28 ibid.
29 ibid.
30 ibid.
31 ibid.
32 ibid.
33 ibid.
34 ibid.
35 ibid.
36 Hamish Freeman to author, July 2008
37 ibid.
38 Rebecca Freeman to author, July 2008
39 Cameron Freeman to author, July 2008

40 ibid.
41 Gavin Lincoln to author, July 2008
42 Sue Bennie to author, July 2008
43 ibid.
44 ibid.
45 Adam Gilchrist to author, August, 2008
46 The Very Reverend Dr John Shepherd, Anglican Dean of Perth, to author, February 2008

Index

Abernathy, Bruce 169, 170
Abley, John 167
Adelaide Crows 14, 122, 170–6,
    186, 189, 193, 195, 197, 227
Alderman, Terry 100, 107
Anderson, Brenton 'Snake' 62
Anderson, Cathy 61
Attenborough, Geoff 153
Australian Story 24, 25–31, 79, 98,
    126, 129, 132, 156, 190
Bampton, Nancy 47
Barlow, Eddie 66, 153
Barnett, Ben 102
Barry Rees Trust Fund 123–6,
    208–11
Barsby, Trevor 151, 154
Bartel, David 181
Barton, Geoff 61, 68
Bassett, Scott 175
Baume, Michael 106, 109
Beard, Donald 'Doc' 16–17, 118
Benaud, Richie 21, 51, 113, 141,
    159, 214
Bennie, Courtney 229
Bennie, Jessie 229
Bennie, Mitchell 229, 230
Bennie, Sue 228–31
Bernard, Steve 154
Berry, Nicholas 206–7, 211
Betro, Ed 176
Bichel, Andy 155
Biglands, Rhett 175
Black, Simon 183
Blewett, Greg 126, 144

Blight, Malcolm 176
Blunden, Terry 177, 178
Bond, Shane 174, 197
Bond, Troy 170, 197
Boon, David 101, 142, 158
Booth, Brian 142
Border, Allan 100–1, 103, 107, 118,
    154
Bowden, Billy 19
Bowyer, W.C. 40, 41
Boyd, Dave 163, 167
Bradley, Craig 168
Bradman, Sir Donald 18, 20, 91,
    102, 107, 121–2, 131, 136,
    141, 144, 146–7, 160, 166,
    206
Brayshaw, Ian 154
Brayshaw, James 124–5, 176
Brebner, Don 166
Brewer, Shayne 174
Brierley, Sir Ron 103, 106, 110–11
Brinsley, Peter 144
Brogan, Dean 188
Brown, Barbara 32
Brown, David 170, 174
Buchanan, John 87, 152
Burdett, Les 150
Burge, Peter 142
Burgoyne, Peter 165, 175, 197
Burgoyne, Shaun 165, 231
Burke, Jim 142
Button, John 26
Cahill, Jack 66, 167, 170–1, 174,
    189

Cairns, Lance 103
Candy, Don 64
Carr, Tom 175
Carter, Stephen 175
Causby, John 80
Chappell, Greg 18, 75, 88, 99–100,
    103, 119, 142, 153, 157
Chappell, Ian 17, 18, 21–2, 37, 50,
    51, 67–8, 75, 83–6, 91, 99,
    103, 120, 123–4, 142, 144,
    153–7, 176
Chappell, Trevor 159
Clarke, Graham 154
Clarke, Michael 'Pup' 16, 152, 154,
    204, 210, 231
Clarke, Stuart 19, 21
Clift, Roger 164
Cochrane, Stewart 184
Colley, David 154
Collinge, Richard 103
Colonel Light Gardens 13, 36–7,
    139, 178, 218
Coney, Jeremy 103
Connolly, Alan 154
Conway, Steve 175
Cornes, Chad 185, 187, 190, 231
Cornes, Graham 170–1, 187
Cornes, Kane 183, 187, 190
Cosier, Gary 99, 142
Cotton, Jarrad 175
Cowdrey, Colin 20, 52, 103, 106
Crusaders 102–15
Cummings, Scott 174
Cunningham, Brian 168
Cunningham, Ken 142, 147–8, 153
Curtin, Barry 154–5, 182
Dale, Adam 151
Daniels, Stephen 175
Dansie, Neil 153
Darling, Mark 154
Davidson, Alan 51, 142, 143, 154,
    214
Davis, Ian 141, 154
Dew, Stuart 175, 184–6
Dickie, Donald 175
Downsborough, Ian 174
Dymock, Geoff 154
Eagleton, Nathan 175
Ebert, Brian 183–4
Ebert, Russell 71–2, 125, 167, 168
Edgar, Bruce 103

Edwards, Ross 142
Egar, Colin 145
Ellenbroek, Hans 14, 81, 86, 125,
    178–81, 224
Elliott, Rob 'Super' 70, 85, 156
Evans, Paul 175
Evans, Tim 168
Evenett, Gwen and John 35
Faehse, Brian 163
Farmer, Graham 'Polly' 165
Favell, Les 21, 50, 53, 66, 67–8,
    77–8, 91, 117, 119–20, 141,
    143–4, 153, 212
Fiacchi, George 170
Fiegert, Nigel 174
Flintoff, Andrew 'Freddy' 89, 153
Francis, Bruce 154
Francis, Fabian 174
Francou, Josh 168–9, 174, 184, 231
Frazer, Ian 102
Freeborne, Scott 175
Freeman, Cameron 13, 168, 226–8
Freeman, Eric 80, 141, 153
Freeman, Hamish 13, 46, 168, 226
Freeman, Neil 13, 94, 97, 115
Freeman, Pam 13, 34, 37–9, 41–2,
    43, 45–6, 91, 94–8, 104, 168,
    214–17, 219, 226
Freeman, Rebecca 13, 226, 227
Frost, Alan 119
Galloway, Paul 80
Geisler, Paul 175
George, Shane 121
Gilchrist, Adam 16, 19, 23, 24,
    27–9, 118, 126, 141, 152,
    153, 155, 156, 196, 209, 212,
    231
Gillespie, Jason 'Dizzy' 14, 18, 123,
    126–8, 142, 143, 153,
    212–13, 222
Ginever, Tim 126, 168, 195–6
Gleeson, John 17, 154
Golding, Phyllis 139–42
Goldsmith, Steve 62
Goodger, Dudley 64
Goodwood Saints Football Club 14,
    178–83, 195, 196, 197
Gott, Doug 106, 111
Grace, W.G. 20, 160
Gray, Marie 61
Greer, Alan 62, 70, 71

greyhound racing 94–7
Grimmett, Clarrie 18, 107, 145
Grout, Wally 55, 67, 141, 214
Gulliver, Fay 61
Guthrie, Eric 42–3
Guthrie, Joyce 42–3, 46
Haddin, Brad 141
Hadlee, Sir Richard 103
Hair, Darryl 150–1
Hammond, Jeff 154
Harley, Ian 26, 30
Harley, Tom 174, 175
Harvey, Neil 141
Harwood, Mark 174
Hastings, Brian 111
Hawke, Bob 100, 103–4, 113
Hawke, Neil 50, 51, 52, 66, 80, 96,
    141, 153
Hayden, Matthew 20–2, 142, 153
Hayes, Neville 'Chicken' 62, 78–80,
    164, 168
Haysman, Michael 100
Healy, Ian 101, 141, 213
Heaver, Brent 174
Hendricks, Mike 154
Heuskes, Adam 175
Higgs, Jimmy 154
Highmore, Stan 112
Hilditch, Andrew 25, 143, 153
Hill, Clem 18
Hoad, Lew 64–5
Hodges, Scott 168, 170
Hogan, Tom 100
Hogg, Rodney 100, 143
Hohns, Trevor 100, 154
Holland, Ben 168
Holland, Nick 168
Hookes, David 75, 82, 103, 118,
    120, 123–6, 128–31, 133,
    141, 153, 176, 212
Hooper, Bob 111–12
Hope Sweeney 81–2
Howard, John 103
Hughes, Kim 100
Hughes, Merv 101, 103, 124, 124,
    141, 176
Hussey, Michael 16, 154, 158
Hutton, David 170
Inverarity, John 25, 27, 30, 130,
    132, 142, 144, 153
Jacobs, Ken 106

James, Roger 175, 184
Jarman, Barry 'BJ' 14, 18, 32,
    48–51, 53, 55–6, 62, 71, 74,
    76, 80, 82–4, 90, 99, 119,
    124, 127, 129, 130, 141, 142,
    144–6, 153, 178, 201, 203–4
    cricket career 62–4, 66–8, 73–4,
    101, 107
Jarman, Gaynor 82, 145
Jenner, Terry 142, 143–4, 147, 153,
    213
Jervis, Lawrie 163
Johnston, Bill 143
Johnston, Mitchell 192
Johnston, Russel 170
Jones, Dean 101, 154
Keily, Keith 42
Keily, Paula 42, 47, 125
Kensington Cricket Club 14, 144–5,
    194–5
Kent, Martin 153
Khan, Younis 134
Kingsley, Adam 192–3
Kline, Lindsay, 'Spinner' 145–6
Kneebone, Harry 168
Kookaburra 85–7, 156, 160, 177
Kooyonga Golf Club 65, 89
Lade, Brendon 175, 188
Laird, Bruce 154
Langer, Justin 141, 153, 158
Lara, Brian 230
Larwood, Harold 18
Law, Stewart 151
Lawry, Bill 63, 142, 154
Lawson, Geoff 101, 107
Lee, Brett 'Binga' 18–22, 126, 142,
    204
Lehmann, Darren 'Uncle Boof' 14,
    28, 100–1, 123, 126, 128–34,
    141, 151, 152, 153, 196, 209,
    213, 223
Lillee, Dennis 20, 28, 81, 99, 107,
    142, 143, 146–7, 153, 155–6,
    157
Lincoln, Gavin 229
Lindwall, Ray 18, 143
Lloyd, Clive 19, 118, 153
Lockwood, Bowen 175
Lyle, Brayden 174
Lynch, Jake 175
McCarthy, Kevin 'Cuan' 84

McCosker, Rick 141
McCurdy, Rod 100
McDermott, Chris 172–3, 195,
    206–11, 227
McDermott, Craig 'Billy the Kid'
    118, 141
McDonald, Bob 15
McDonald, Harold 164
MacGill, Stuart 'Macgilla' 141–2,
    154
McGrath, Glenn 'Pigeon' 16, 20,
    143, 147
McGregor, Ken 64
McGuinness, Tony 'Freddie' 14,
    122–5, 171–3, 176, 187,
    189–91, 193, 195, 206–11,
    215
McGuinness-McDermott
    Foundation 173, 176, 206–8,
    222
McGuire, John 100
McIntyre, Peter 88, 103, 105, 111,
    121, 223
Mackay, Ken 154
McKenzie, Graham 154
MacKinnon, John 105, 113
McLay, Mark 31
McLean, Bob 163–7
MacLean, John 154
McLean, Nathan 206–7, 211
McLelland, Doug 113
Mallett, Ashley 141, 153
Malone, Mick 154
Mann, Tony 154
Manou, Graham 141
Marks, Lynn 'Full' 136, 154
Marks, Neil 'Harpo' 136, 154,
    159–60
Marsh, Geoff 101
Marsh, Rodney 80–1, 99, 141, 142,
    154, 157
Marshall, Malcolm 103
Martin, Johnny 51, 154
Matthews, Scott 175
May, Fred 62–3
May, Tim 101, 107, 118, 142
Mead, Darren 175
Meckiff, Ian 145
Millard, Hugh 77
Miller, Keith 'Nugget' 18, 48, 107,
    143, 154

Mitchell, Ron 41
Moody, Tom 101
Morrison, John 103
Motley, Geof 70–2, 162, 166,
    167
Motley, Peter 72
Moyle, Phil 62
Moyle, Russell 58–9, 61, 76, 77, 79,
    99, 168
Munn, Darby 77
Murilitharan, Muttiah 150, 152
Mutton, Howard 154
Muzurke, Marg 61
Nelsen, Tiny 178
Newbery, Len 102, 103
Nielsen, Tim 14, 88
Nugget's Bat Oil 69–70
Oatley, Jack 166
O'Keeffe, Kerry 120, 154
O'Neill, Norm 51, 66–7, 142,
    145–6, 154
O'Reilly, Bill 18, 107
Osborne, Andrew 175
Page, Wendy 25, 26–31, 61, 126,
    132, 183, 190, 201
Palmerston Lass 94–6
Papandrea, John 62, 168
Parker, John 144
Parkinson, David 'DH' 134, 144,
    178
Parkinson, Michael 103
Parkinson, Sam 144, 153, 176–9,
    210
Parkinson Blunden 177–80
Pascoe, Len 154
Patching, Kylie 31
Paxman, Steven 174
Perry, Mike 182
Pettigrew, Michael 189
Phillips, Greg 168, 170
Phillips, Wayne 153
Pickett, Byron 165
Pollock, Graeme 66
Ponsford, Bill 18
Ponting, Ricky 'Punter' 16–21,
    127, 152, 153, 158, 204,
    210, 231
Poole, Darryl 175
Port Adelaide Magpies 14, 66, 71,
    78, 84, 91, 136, 162–7,
    169–76, 189–90, 193–6, 197

Port Power 14, 32, 70, 136, 165, 174–5, 181–9, 193, 195–6, 197, 203, 230–1
Potter, Jeff 167
Primus, Matthew 174, 193
Prior, Wayne 153
Queen Elizabeth II 108–14
Quinn, Paul 111
Rackermann, Carl 100, 101, 151, 154
Radiant Robert 40–1
Raggatt, David 62
Redpath, Ian 142
Rees, Barry 'Nugget'
  animals 40–1, 96–7
  baggy green 67, 145–6, 160, 185
  birth 34–6
  childhood 36–43
  fame 97–9, 123
  lawn mowing 90–1
  manners 14, 15, 43, 53–4, 60, 133, 139, 219–20
  memory 59, 60, 79
  methodical nature 55–6, 70
  motivational speeches 21–3, 85, 87–8, 130–1, 133, 155, 158–59, 183, 186, 190–1
  perceptive nature 17, 60–1, 72, 132, 152, 191
  respect 14, 23, 73, 133, 219–20
  spirituality and kindness 26, 31, 41, 125, 139, 156, 228–32
  teacher, as 200–2
Rees, Diane see Smith, Diane
Rees, Isabel Beatrice Maud 43
Rees, Mary 34, 39, 42, 45
Rees, Pam see Freeman, Pam
Rees, Ray 13, 34, 35, 39, 40, 43–8, 50, 51, 66, 83–4, 90, 94, 104, 162, 164, 173, 204, 214, 215, 221–5
Rees, William 'Bill' 36, 42, 43, 47, 66, 162, 164, 173
Rees, William Griffith 43
Renfrey, Steve 125
Rice, Sir Tim 103
Richards, Barry 68, 120, 153
Richards, Bob 'Swan' 55, 73–8, 83, 86, 100, 102–15
Richards, David 102
Richards, Joan 105, 112

Richardson, Matthew 194–5
Richardson, Vic 18
Ridings, Phil 'Pancho' 85
Ritchie, Greg 141, 154
Rixon, Steve 154
Robbins, Wendy 61
Roberts, Les 42
Robertson, Trevor 83
Rombotis, John 174
Rosewall, Ken 64–5
Rowe, Betty 65
Rowe, David 'Tidd' 14, 48–50, 55, 62, 64–5, 68, 76, 85, 89–90, 99, 102, 115, 124, 178, 201, 203, 222
Rowe, Ernie 64
Rowe, Florence 64
Rowe, Mike 60
Rowe, Walter Tidd 64
Rowe & Jarman 14, 48–50, 52, 54–6, 58–60, 61–2, 65, 68–71, 73, 76, 78, 81, 83–4, 99, 101–2, 122, 136, 171, 176, 187, 201, 203–5, 225, 229
Ruess, Rudolph 45–6
Ruess, Theresa 45–6, 105, 215, 217, 223
Russell, Richard 168
Salopek, Stephen 186
'same day service' 54–5, 80
Saunders, John 62
Schultz, Sally 202–4
Schultz, Steve 202–6
Schulz, Jan 61
Sellers, Rex 'Sahib' 119, 153
Sheahan, Paul 141, 154, 157
Sheedy, Kevin 174, 189, 193, 208, 214
Shepherd, Barry 143–4
Shepherd, Rev Dr John 25–7, 29, 232
Shiell, Alan 153
Shipperd, Greg 100
Siddons, Jamie 120, 151
Simmons, Jack 163, 164
Simpson, Bobby 67, 101, 154, 159
Sims, Dennis 176
Sincock, David 153
Slater, Keith 154
Slee, Arthur 'Slugger' 59–60, 61, 69, 76, 77, 99, 168

Sleep, Peter 144
Slowdown football match 208
Small, Gladstone 103
Smith, Cassie 13, 181, 215, 217, 220–1
Smith, Corey 13, 168, 215, 217–20
Smith, Darren 168, 170
Smith, Diane 13, 29, 34, 37, 39, 43, 45, 104–5, 112, 115, 121, 168, 188, 195, 196, 204, 208–9, 214–26
Smith, Rusty 13, 105, 115, 208–9, 215–17, 221–2
Smythe, Greg 87
Sobers, Garry 20, 50, 117, 119, 153
South Australian Trotting Association 40, 44
Squires, Damien 175
Steele, Ray 102
Steinberner, Nathan 175
Stevens, Laurie 164
Stoddart, Andrew 62
Surjen, Jacob 187
Symonds, Andrew 'Roy' 19, 21–2, 192, 211
Taber, Brian 67, 141, 154
Tait, Shaun 143
Tallon, Don 25, 101
Tannock, Taylor 31
Taylor, John 109–10, 113
Taylor, Mark 'Tubby' 18, 21, 101, 152
Taylor, Michael 100
team feeling 22–3
Tebbutt, Amye 31
Tendulkar, Sachin 127, 213–14
Tessesrie, Don 62
Thomas, Charlie 180
Thomson, Jeff 20, 81, 99, 142, 143, 153
Tierney, Ken 164
Tredrea, Warren 174, 182, 185–6
Tregenza, Simon 170, 174

Trumper, Victor 18
Turner, Alan 154
Usher, Jane 61
Usher, Matt 102
Van der Merwve, Peter 64
Vievers, Tom 142
Walker, Max 103, 141
Walkerville Under-12s 168
Walsh, Courtney 118
Walters, Doug 67, 85, 99, 141, 148, 153, 156
Wanganeen, Gavin 165, 174, 214
Warne, Shane 14, 16, 20, 103, 118, 134, 143, 147, 150, 153, 212
Watson, Graeme 154
Waugh, Dean 144
Waugh, Mark 'Junior' 118, 142, 143, 149, 154, 212
Waugh, Steve 'Tugga' 15, 22, 28, 101, 107, 123–8, 142, 143, 152, 154, 176, 213, 217
Weber, Bruce 169
Webster, Don 62
Weston, Paul 62, 102
Whelan, Ted 164, 167
Williams, Foster 66, 162–6, 167, 189
Williams, Mark 66, 181, 183, 189–93, 214
Williams, Steven 66, 170, 173, 176, 189
Wilson, John 119–20
Wilson, Michael 188
Wilson, Paul 151
Woodcock, Ashley 153
Woolley, Michael 47
Woolmer, Bob 64
Wykes, Ted 149–50
Yardley, Bruce 154
Yebury, Jonathon 174
Young, Brad 151–2
Younger, John 105
Zucker, Lloyd 164